LOVE TACTICS

How to Win the One You Want

www.lovetactics.com

THOMAS W. McKNIGHT
ROBERT H. PHILLIPS

SQUAREONE
PUBLISHERS

Cover Designer: Phaedra Mastrocola
In-House Editor: Marie Caratozzolo
Typesetter: Gary A. Rosenberg

Square One Publishers
Garden City Park, NY 11040
www.squareonepublishers.com

Library of Congress Cataloging-in-Publication Data

McKnight, Thomas W.
    Love tactics : how to win the one you want / Thomas W. McKnight,
Robert H. Phillips.
        p. cm.
Originally published: Garden City Park, N.Y. : Avery Pub. Group, c1988.
    ISBN 0-7570-0037-1
    1. Love.   2. Courtship—United States.   I. Phillips, Robert H., 1948–
II. Title.
    HQ801 .M488 2002
    646.7'7—dc21
                                                            2001057827

Printed in Canada

10   9   8   7   6

Contents

Acknowledgments

To Charles and Alois McKnight, whose commitment and love for one another has shown the way; to Rudy Shur, without whose confidence this message of hope might never have been so widely shared; to Marie Caratozzolo, our editor, who brilliantly found the words to give this work added life; to Gaylynn, the one worth waiting for; and most of all, to God, who is the true and ultimate source of all love.

—TWM

This book is dedicated to all those wonderful people—family and friends—who have always been there for me, providing love and support when I needed it, and sharing progress and growth together.

I must acknowledge the participation of Sharon Balaban and Jacqueline Balla for their patience and expertise in processing, editing, and preparing this project.

—RHP

Introduction

The reason is very clear why *Love Tactics* has become a perennial bestseller over the last two decades. Why? The answer is painfully obvious to anyone who has ever felt the agonizing frustration of not having their love reciprocated.

Isn't it ironic that in spite of the many technological advances made within the last century, people today are still as frustrated as ever in their quest for true love? Our society is full of individuals who have disappointedly abandoned their idealistic dreams of romantic fulfillment. It almost seems a law of nature that the one *you* want never wants you back, while the ones who *are* interested in you are simply incapable of stirring your emotions! Love forever looms on the horizon, but is just out of reach.

Many have given up, deciding that nothing can be done to alter an apparently loveless destiny. They have resigned themselves to going through life, taunted by the prospects of love, but never truly possessing it. You may have experienced such feelings of helplessness yourself. If so, then this book is the answer to your prayers.

Love Tactics demonstrates why there is a very real reason not to give up hope. Love is *not* the mere result of chance meetings determined by pure luck. Believe it or not, love is a *predictable human response!* It results whenever a person's key psychological needs are satisfied. It's true that, on occasion, love does seem to occur accidentally. But even in these cases, such relationships still conform to the principles of romantic behavior outlined in this book. Anyone who chooses to consciously apply these rules of love in an intelligent manner need not go through life unloved. Succeeding in romance, then, only requires becoming aware of your ability to modify and influence the emotional moods, attitudes, and behaviors of others through well-proven psychological techniques. We're not talking about taking unfair advantages—just using strategic common sense!

As you can probably imagine, it would be impossible to include all the different strategies, techniques, and tips that can possibly be used in winning the one you want. So *Love Tactics* provides the basic formula from which you will be able to derive your own solution to your particular circumstances. As you read the book, you'll find yourself becoming more enthusiastic, confident, and eager to approach others in your goal to win the person of your dreams.

Divided into two main sections, *Love Tactics* presents dozens of techniques that are designed to help you in the most exciting search-and-succeed activities of your life. These strategies, which are found in Part One, will help you win the love of that special someone. Part Two goes a step further by helping those who feel they have already found their love, but have lost or are in danger of losing that person. How to win *back* another person's love is the theme of this section.

Not all of the strategies found in *Love Tactics* are suitable for every situation. Different approaches work better than others, depending on the particular need of the moment. Experience will help you see which tactics are best suited for different conditions. Nonetheless, you'll also learn that certain fundamental principles of psychology *always* apply, and are the basis for your selection of tactics.

You must nurture friendship, respect, and passion in order to win the heart of the one you want. This fundamental understanding is the bedrock foundation of the *Love Tactics* strategy, and the way to ultimately win. Trust that if you cultivate the relationship properly, you will ultimately reap a magnificent harvest!

Of the many lessons you'll learn in *Love Tactics*, remember this important truth above all else: *The way to true love is not to sit back and wait for the person of your dreams to magically appear. Rather, it involves choosing the one you want above all others, and then winning them over using known principles of human romantic behavior.*

Yes, you *can* win the one you want! You can also win *back* the one you've lost! You don't have to settle for anything (or anyone) less. The dream is in sight! It's merely a matter of psychology. *Love Tactics* will acquaint you with the science of human behavior as it relates to love and romance, and teach you how to *win the one you want!*

PART ONE

Winning the One You Want

*I*t's time to learn the "tricks of the trade" in cultivating your love object's desire for you. Your goal? To plant the longing for a lifelong partnership in that person. The love tactics presented in Part One are strategies that will help you to achieve this goal.

Succeeding in a relationship is like succeeding in anything else. Knowledge is power! The better you understand what makes a relationship tick, the better you can make it work. Remember this: There is always a reason why a relationship succeeds or fails. If you don't understand what has gone wrong in past relationships, then you're still at the mercy of fate. A clear and accurate understanding of what went wrong is vital to your future success! So the key to romantic success is knowledge. The strategies offered in the following chapters are designed to help you to gain that knowledge.

1

General Strategy

*T*he general strategy behind *Love Tactics* is quite simple. It is based on the premise that romantic love has three essential parts: 1. *Friendship*, 2. *Respect*, and 3. *Passion*. Because the recipe for love will fail if it lacks one or more of these necessary ingredients, the only way to be successful in winning the one you want is by learning how to encourage and cultivate *all three* such feelings for you in the heart of that person.

THE HOUSE OF LOVE

We can compare a love relationship to a housing unit. As long as it is complete and functions the way it should, it makes a pleasant abode. There is no incentive for those who are enjoying the home to move out or abandon the premises, since all their needs for shelter and comfort are being adequately met.

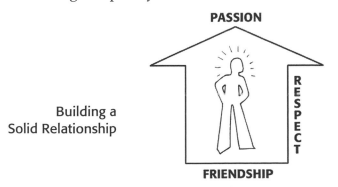

Building a
Solid Relationship

But what if the resident came home night after night, only to discover that there was no roof? Or floor? Or walls? It wouldn't be long before that person would be looking for a new home!

Out of desperation, some people may jump prematurely into a situation that meets one of their more immediate superficial needs. But if this situation doesn't satisfy their other important emotional requirements as well, they will eventually realize their mistake—and move out!

Why does love sometimes fail? In most cases it can be traced to the absence of one or more of these three essential elements, which, together, contain all the ingredients necessary for the development of romantic fulfillment. Just as a house would be incomplete without a roof, walls, or a foundation, so would a relationship be unfulfilling without friendship, respect, and passion. If just one of these components fails to germinate and develop in either party, then the person lacking these feelings for the other cannot help but feel a little dissatisfied (yes, even cheated). The relationship would be about as rewarding as sitting down on a three-legged stool and finding out too late that it has only two legs!

The basic strategy, then, to win *and keep* the one you want is to cultivate friendship, respect, and passion in your relationship with that person. Only when all three of these essential elements are present can you hope to enjoy love at its very best.

Friendship

A wise person once defined a *friend* as "someone you can think out loud in front of." (In light of this definition, then, we might all find ourselves reevaluating who we really consider to be our true friends.) Before you can truly win someone's heart, you must first become genuine friends with that person. Although this may appear easy, it really is not. True friendship involves meeting a person's deep emotional needs. So, what are these basic needs? And how can you best meet them in the eyes of the one you want?

1. **Attention.** Show the person that you are consciously aware of his or her existence.

2. **Understanding.** Demonstrate your sincerity in striving to identify with how that person feels about and perceives the surrounding world.

3. **Acceptance.** Even though the person's behavior or attitudes may be less than praiseworthy at times, use a non-critical demeanor to assure his or her value to you.

4. **Appreciation.** Openly acknowledge those praiseworthy qualities that the other person possesses.

5. **Affection.** Regardless of how the person might compare with others, make it clear that he or she is still very special to you and, therefore, very important. Sometimes this reassurance can be communicated by no more than a simple touch.

As you begin to meet these basic emotional friendship needs, you'll be helping that person along the road to greater happiness. In return, he or she will develop a subconscious emotional dependence on you. This dependency is an essential part of any romantic relationship. However, in order to encourage that person to voluntarily place this trust in you, you must first prove worthy of that trust.

BEHAVIOR PRINCIPLE #1

*People Subconsciously Grow Dependent
Upon Those Who Satisfy Their Emotional Needs.*

The first objective of *Love Tactics* is to show you how to satisfy the emotional friendship needs of the one you want—and to do it better and more completely than anyone this person has ever met before. The various techniques presented throughout this book will help you accomplish this.

Respect

While it is true that pure friendship is the engine of romantic love, *respect* is the gas that makes it go. People are motivated to be with and to associate themselves with those persons whom they truly respect.

How do we come to respect someone? Respect is an acquired attitude. For the most part, it is usually based on our perception of a person's independence and self-reliance. The more capable a person seems of getting along in life without having to rely on another, the more likely we are to actually feel drawn towards that person. The opposite also holds true. The more easily a person becomes dependent upon us, the more "turned off" we tend to become. When people act possessive and show an inclination to "cling," our degree of respect for them has a tendency to decline. It is quite normal to feel a need to escape from such persons.

BEHAVIOR PRINCIPLE #2

*People Are Most Attracted to Those Who Exhibit
Some Degree of Aloofness and Emotional Independence.*

If you want to win someone's heart fully and completely, you must be perceived by that person as being capable of surviving quite well without him or her. At the same time, you cannot neglect the person's very real psychological need for friendship. This presents you with the task of performing a delicate balancing act of befriending someone while retaining a certain air of aloofness. Again, *Love Tactics* will show you how to accomplish both objectives simultaneously.

Passion

The crowning experience of romantic love is the ultimate sensation we know as *passion*. We can enjoy something in life only to the degree that we truly long for it. Therefore, levels of romantic desire must be raised to a fever pitch if the romantic experience is really going to satisfy the need for a fulfilling relationship and become the ecstasy we have always dreamed of. This brings us to one of the most widely known but sadly misapplied principles of human behavior:

BEHAVIOR PRINCIPLE #3

People Want What They Can't Have!

What happens when people become overly confident that a desirable object is "theirs for the taking?" They usually take such a treasure for granted. (Frequently, they'll even abuse it!) Therefore, if you want to build a successful romantic relationship with someone, it is imperative to pay attention to this principle. Otherwise, you will wind up forfeiting the rewards that you could have ultimately reaped.

The secret to building passion in another person can be expressed in the form of a mathematical equation:

HOPE + DOUBT = PASSION

By using the tactics discussed throughout this book, you can build a romantic fire in someone else's heart that will blaze exclusively for you. Once begun, this fire will burn so brightly that the embers will continue to glow for a lifetime! So there is no time like the present to concentrate on fueling that fire.

Commitment

Falling in love is ultimately a rational, conscious act. It's a willful decision to let down one's last remaining emotional barriers and become wholly vulnerable to another human being. But even though this final decision to become vulnerable is a rational one, it is almost always based upon subconscious motives (of which the person falling in love is hardly aware). As financier J.P. Morgan reportedly once quipped, "Every man has two reasons for doing or not doing a thing: One that sounds good, and a real one."

BEHAVIOR PRINCIPLE #4

People Make Conscious Decisions Based on Subconscious Feelings, Then Justify Their Decisions with Reasons That Sound Good.

It is this principle that explains why people often feel that they are "falling" in love, rather than realizing that they are actually "choosing" to be in love. Most people are unaware of the factors that subconsciously contribute to their decision to be in love with another person. However, by becoming aware of and using the emotional factors that will contribute to someone else's reason to be in love, it will be a fairly simple matter of setting them up to "fall" in love with you.

It doesn't matter how *logical* it may seem that a particular person should be in love with you. If the proper emotional attitudes have not been cultivated within that person, then a meaningful commitment simply will not occur. It is true that a person may commit to you based on sheer will power alone; but typically, that person will also feel a void and emptiness inside, undermining the strength of his or her commitment to you in the long run.

On the other hand, if the proper feelings of friendship, respect, and passion have been appropriately cultivated in the relationship, it would be much more difficult for the person to resist making such a commitment to you, regardless of all the "logical" reasons he or she shouldn't.

PATIENCE AND THE CORRECT APPROACH

The laws of behavior assure that there is no person whose heart cannot be won, given the correct approach and enough time to apply the proper strategy.

One of our readers, Dr. Ed Waldrip, shared one of his childhood experiences with us. While growing up on his grandfather's farm in Louisiana, young Ed was in awe of one of the hired hands—a wise old mule-skinner named Zelmer Jackson—who tamed mules and horses that were often considered "untrainable." Zelmer's reputation for accomplishing miracles with these "lost causes" was well deserved, but his accomplishments were really not miraculous—they were the direct result of his effective training method.

On the first day of training, old Zelmer would fill a bucket with "all grain" and carry it into the pasture. He would then set the bucket on the ground near the animal. Eventually, even the most unruly horse or mule ventured over to the bucket to sample its contents. While the animal ate, Zelmer slowly approached it while carrying an old burlap feedbag. When he was close enough, Zelmer attempted to rub down the animal with the bag. Of course, the skittish animal often bolted a few yards away. When it did, Zelmer immediately picked up the bucket of grain and returned to the barn.

Zelmer repeated the process every day, and each day, the animal became a little less anxious and a little more secure around this man with the bucket of delicious grain. It didn't take long for the animal to learn that in order to get the grain, it had to accept being rubbed down. In some cases, this took many weeks, and even longer before the animal allowed Zelmer to fit it with a harness. Zelmer would start by placing one piece of harness at a time on the animal's back. Again, if the animal shied away, Zelmer picked up the bucket and headed back to the barn.

Even the wildest mule or horse learned two things: First, if it wanted the grain, it had to accept Zelmer's terms; and second, the terms really weren't so bad. Eventually, Zelmer was able to harness the animals, which were then used to pull wooden sleds filled with supplies through areas that were too rough for wheeled carts to go.

Once trained, the animals provided faithful service to Zelmer, who, in turn, never failed to reward them with daily buckets of grain.

"I never saw an animal that didn't respond to this treatment," Waldrip testified to us. Patience and persistence were the keys to Zelmer's success. The love tactics presented in this book use the same approach. No matter how wild and unachievable you may think the one you want is, remember that patience and persistence, when used appropriately, can be the key to romantic success. And love is your bucket of grain, which comes in the form of attention, understanding, acceptance, appreciation, and affection.

LOVE IS YOURS FOR THE TAKING

If it's your desire to truly be loved by the one you want—if your goal is to achieve a complete, fulfilling, and totally reciprocated commitment from the person of your dreams—then get smart! Cultivate friendship, respect, and passion in your relationship, and you will see how commitment will follow as naturally as day follows night.

The general strategy of this book is based on the philosophy that "love begets love." The key is to communicate that love. It begins with your commitment to love another human being, and ends with that person's commitment to love you back. And once you have found the one you want—that special person with whom you'd like to develop a romantic, committed relationship—the love tactics and methods presented in the following chapters will help guide you on your mission. By applying these tactics faithfully and consistently, you will be surprised at how easy it really is to win the one you want.

2

Acting with Self-Assurance

Principle: *People are most readily drawn to those who radiate a positive self-image.*

---

ow you're ready to begin! You're willing to give it a try and pursue the one you want. You realize that this book will finally unravel the mystery of how to do it. But deep down, you're still wondering if you've got what it takes. You have self-doubts. You're afraid.

Dispel those fears! It's true that this whole process begins with you, but we have faith in you! We know from personal experience that no matter who you are, within you lies an untapped capacity to succeed in this undertaking. All you need is a little direction. We haven't the slightest doubt that your true greatness will become apparent as you begin to use love tactics.

This chapter contains a number of tactics that will help you feel confident about yourself. As this confidence grows, you will become more emotionally prepared to successfully win the one you want. Additionally, you will radiate more charm to help enchant and draw that person to you.

Whitney Houston sings that "learning to love yourself is the greatest love of all." It is understandable that, unless you feel good about yourself, you cannot show much love to another person. Therefore, it's important to like yourself as much as possible—you need a "positive self-image."

VIBES

Have you ever noticed that people tend to pick up vibes from those around them? Think about the people you enjoy being with the most. Undoubtedly, they send out positive vibes, and that's why you enjoy their company. Doesn't it make sense to radiate these same vibes to others? But how is this done? Again, by feeling good about yourself.

A positive self-image gives off positive vibes, which are apparent in your face, your speech, and your general behavior. These vibes become an "aura" that brightens the atmosphere around you, engulfing and captivating those with whom you come into contact. People will enjoy being with you because of your positive attitude. This is the true source of that personal magnetism known as *charisma.*

❤ 1 *Be Nice to Yourself*

Before you can begin to glow with self-confidence, you must start treating yourself with kindness, tolerance, and mercy. Many people are harder on themselves than they need to be. They are too negative and self-critical in their private thoughts. Constantly bad-mouthing yourself will serve only to keep your self-image low. And, consequently, such self-depreciation can also diminish your ability to win the one you want.

So cut it out! As a first step toward winning the one you want, commit yourself here and now to break these patterns of self-abuse. Make up your mind to stop putting yourself down. From now on, it is essential that you go easier on yourself and be nice to Number One (yes, that's you!) True, you may not be perfect, but it is vital to the overall plan that you at least treat yourself with respect.

How do you begin if such self put-downs are already a habit? First, become aware of exactly how often you exercise this harmful behavior. Take note whenever you say something negative to yourself. Mentally keep track of your self-dialogues and personal thoughts. What did you say? What were your reasons for being upset with yourself?

Even if you get angry at something you've done, realize that you can learn from your mistakes. You *can* change. Criticize your behavior instead of blaming yourself. Emphasize the action rather than the person. It is so much better to say, "I made a mistake," rather than, "I'm a loser!" Turn those negatives around! You can always find something positive about yourself.

Sure, this requires letting yourself off the hook sometimes when you blow it. But who doesn't deserve a good dose of mercy from time to time? And we promise that the improvement you will see in yourself because of this new attitude will surpass any results you can achieve through chastisement! You'll gradually improve the way you feel about yourself. As you feel more confident, it will begin to show, and the people around you will respond to that positive aura you radiate.

This is not to say that you should engage in the practice of excusing your faults or bragging to others. Just realize that everyone has faults. Making mistakes does not make you a "bad" person. In fact, being human can actually work in your favor. As someone once said, "I don't want someone who is *too* perfect!" The truth is that nobody is perfect. Everyone makes mistakes and, heck, you are certainly entitled to your share. Mistakes do not make a person inferior—only human!

Don't become discouraged if you're having a hard time shaking your feelings of inferiority. Be aware that if you are plagued with a bit of an inferiority complex, you are not alone. In fact, most people secretly feel inferior to others, although they don't go around broadcasting this. So your feelings of inadequacy are not the end of the world. You can *still* win the one you want, in spite of it. Millions have. But the more accepting you are of yourself (without putting yourself down), the greater your advantage.

Put past negative behaviors where they belong—in the past. Realize that no matter what frailties you may have exhibited, if you are capable of recognizing them as faults, you possess the capacity to improve yourself.

Make an effort to control your inner thinking. Indulging in negative thoughts can be one of the most destructive things you do. How do you know you're thinking negatively? By your feelings! Whenever you're feeling depressed, angry, guilty, lonely, sad, hopeless, or any other unsettling emotion, you can be sure there are negative thoughts on your mind. These feelings may sometimes be subconscious; however, try to get them out in the open! Ask yourself, "What exactly am I feeling?" "Why am I feeling this way?" "What specific incidents are making me feel this way?"

You can't stop feelings and impressions from popping into your head, but you can certainly control how you react to them! Practice the "red flag" approach. Identify negative thoughts as soon as they appear in your mind—in essence, red flag them. As soon as you're aware that they exist, defuse them. Face them squarely. Examine them and analyze them for what they are. Be thorough. Be exhaustive. Take several days to do this, if necessary, and then write those thoughts down. Ask yourself which of those negative thoughts can be changed, and which ones cannot. Then attempt to change the ones that can, and accept the ones that cannot.

You may feel bad that you can't change everything in your life, but you'll be surprised at how much better you'll feel just by changing the few things you *do* have control over. This will greatly increase your self-esteem and subsequently heighten your ability to win the one you want.

GIVE YOURSELF CREDIT

Of course, the best thing you can do to boost your self-esteem is to realize the many good things you already have going for you. What are your good qualities? What are the positive aspects of you, the person? Everyone has them. Think about yours. Again, sit down with a pencil and paper and compile a list of your good qualities. At first, you might feel like you don't have any (or very few). But that's not true. Every person has positive traits, and you owe it to yourself to recognize yours. Once you get started, you'll be surprised at how your list will continue to grow.

Think about the positives in your life—your abilities, your accomplishments. Identify the people who like you, the people who look up to and respect you. Write down all of the aspects of yourself that *you* actually like, including character traits, talents, and achievements. Write down the nice things you have done for others, any acts of kindness you can remember showing. Write down the skills you possess naturally or have developed. Read over the list—you'll be surprised at the effect it will have on your self-esteem. It will make you feel good about yourself, maybe better than you have felt in a long time!

Even after you've completed this exercise and have moved on to other parts of this book, continue adding to your list of positives. Make this an ongoing "work in progress" that you add to throughout your life. Tuck it away in a drawer to review and revise from time to time. Benjamin Franklin did this, and he believed that it helped him continually improve himself. When you're feeling down or suffering from a shaky self-image, take out this list and review it. It can help you feel better.

Try to remember these two effective ways to improve your self-image—*thinking positively* and *identifying your positive characteristics*. And as your self-acceptance manifests itself, others will follow your lead and become more accepting of you.

② *Identify Your Goals*

Something very strange happens when you start to center your life—and happiness—on another person. Things get out of kilter, out of whack. Oddly enough, even though there is no greater joy than that of being loved by another person, as soon as the gratification of that need becomes the primary focus of your life, it will elude you. It is paradoxical, but true, that in order to successfully win someone's love and devotion, you must first learn how to be happy *without* their love and devotion—at least to some degree. Happy relationships seldom result from the joining of two unhappy people. They arise from the union of two happy individuals. This means that your best chance of possessing the love you've always dreamed of will come from pursuing your own destiny and attempting to find as much personal satisfaction and happiness as you can on your own—alone. As you do this, love will follow *you.* In this regard, love is like a shadow. It runs from you when chased directly, but when you give up on it and turn to walk away, it will be found tagging along behind you.

Not long ago, we prodded a friend, asking when he and his girlfriend were going to get around to "tying the knot." The friend suddenly became very sober and frankly admitted that something was lacking in his attitude towards his girl. "She's great," he said, "but it seems like she has no goals in life other than to get married. I'm beginning to feel as if I need somebody more goal-oriented!"

Most people are subconsciously drawn to those who have clearly defined goals and objectives—without the influence of anyone else! You, too, must establish a course of direction if you hope to attract the one you want. Pursuing your own destiny, however, requires identifying your own set of personal goals and then planning ways to achieve them. Having goals and anticipating the steps necessary to meet them are essential processes for happy and successful living.

Goal setting can be a very encouraging experience. It focuses on your positive potential, rather than your negative deficiencies. This, in itself, will reassure you of your true limitless value and help you convey greater self-confidence to others. Have you ever been concerned that the one you want might not desire you because you lack certain qualities? Then improvement in these areas should be among your goals. And your self confidence will continue to in crease as you feel yourself meeting these goals.

But perhaps the greatest benefit of identifying goals and planning ways to achieve them is the sense of power that comes from actively taking steps to assume control of your own life. Think about those times when you've felt good about yourself. Now compare them to the times when you didn't. In most cases, you were probably feeling good when you were proactive in achieving something. On the other hand, when you sat around doing nothing, were bored, or passively hoped for something to happen, you probably felt much less positive about yourself. Without definite goals to work towards, you'll stagnate and lose confidence in yourself, floundering aimlessly. (The last thing you need to impress the one you want, right?) Goals help you to determine direction, so you can proceed with confidence!

Picture the following scenario: Your car is filled with gas. You start the ignition, shift into gear, and pull out of your parking space. All of a sudden you realize, "I don't know where I'm going!" Sounds strange, doesn't it? Yet many of us are content to do this day after day with a vehicle that is much more precious than any car—our very lives! Don't fall into this trap! *Love Tactics* demands that you take a more active role in the management of your own life. The following list will help you identify your personal goals and take steps to achieve them.

1. **Decide what you want.** Think about your present wishes and desires. Dream big, but break your dream down into small steps. This way, you will steadily progress towards your goal. Ask yourself, "What exactly do I want to accomplish in the near future? What do I want to achieve?" Make sure your goals consist of things that you, personally, can work towards. Don't depend on the whims of others to help you achieve your ambitions. Remember, you can't depend on somebody else to accomplish your goals for you. You're the only one you can count on to implement your plan.

2. **Write down your goals.** For some reason, goals tend to become more achievable the moment they are written down. A concrete list also provides a record, which will help you keep track of your progress. Otherwise, it's far too easy to forget your goals and not follow through.

3. **Know your priorities.** Of the many goals you would like to accomplish, decide which ones are the most important. This will help you determine which ones to work towards first.

4. **Attach a time frame.** Unlike a wish, a goal has a time frame within which it should be accomplished.

5. **Break your goals down into daily tasks.** When we talk about setting goals, we don't just mean those that are long term, but also
those that are to be met each day. How effective is a teacher who
is concerned with the semester exam, but neglects planning the
daily lessons? You will be most effective by breaking down your
long-term goals into shorter-term, more immediate objectives.

Deciding on a specific plan—forming goals and planning the
steps necessary to achieve each one—is one of the most essential
processes for happy and successful living. Do it! As you will eventually discover, it will assist you in winning the one you want.

 *Relax!*

Anyone who has ever had a really serious crush on someone is aware
of the tension and anxiety associated with simply being in the same
room with that person. You think you're just about going to die,
right? Your legs feel like putty, and you're afraid to speak because
you're sure you'll only be able to manage a hoarse whisper (with a
couple of squeaks thrown in for good measure!). Your instincts tell
you to hide this nervousness, while your good sense says that you
can't—and this only heightens the tension you are feeling! What's a
self-respecting person supposed to do in a situation like this? Why,
relax, of course. You may be thinking that this is easier said than
done. You've never been able to master the art of relaxation. Today,
though, you are going to learn something that will be more helpful to
you than all the relaxation exercises in the world. Are you ready!
Here it is: *It's okay to be nervous!* Did you get that? Let's go over it one
more time, because it's a hard concept to grasp: *It's okay to be nervous!*
That's right! The very thing we go around trying to avoid all our
lives is not so terrible after all.

The real problem isn't your nervousness, but your unwillingness
to forge ahead with your plans in spite of it! Actually, the power to
succeed has been in you all along, but you've been deceived into
avoiding it. So relax. Realize that it's okay to be nervous. You'd be
surprised to learn how many people will actually be *more* attracted to

you when they sense your courage to act in spite of your fears. A shaky voice is music to their ears and a greater compliment than you can imagine. This doesn't mean you have to discuss your nervousness. Don't go to any unnatural extremes to either suppress it *or* enhance it. Just be willing to go with the flow. You might as well experience it while you can, in fact, because it won't last. Once you start acting in spite of your fears, your nervousness will soon begin to dissipate. Would you like to know the most effective cure for nervousness? It's experience.

Now why is it important to relax and accept any nervousness as part of your quest for the one you want? Well, obviously, you want to feel that you're making the best possible impression, right? The best way to impress someone is to be natural—*be yourself.* This includes letting your nervousness show, if it's real. Just don't fail to act because of it. *That* would be the bigger mistake. Being able to relax and accept yourself as is can be a very important tool in helping you feel in control of the situation. By finding an inner calm and peace in your quiet, reflective moments alone, you'll realize that your entire world doesn't depend on a single encounter with another person. You'll find inner resources of self-confidence that you can fall back on whenever your anxiety level would otherwise be reaching the "red zone."

There's another reason for being accepting of yourself when you're with others. Conveying a self-accepting demeanor helps others to follow your lead and feel calm and relaxed *with you.* On the one hand, if you place too much importance on every rendezvous and constantly exhibit dissatisfaction with your own nervousness, it is likely to produce uneasiness in the person who is with you. This may encourage that individual to become a little more defensive and "on guard." On the other hand, the more carefree and relaxed you are, the freer your subconscious mind will be to guide your actions in social settings. And, like an automatic homing device, you'll find that trusting your intuitive powers will lead you where you want to go, in spite of your initial nervousness.

Of course, most people perform best when they are relaxed and anxiety-free. But how, you ask, can you possibly keep from freezing up during important situations? The answer: You can't! So if you've blown a situation, don't feel distraught. Consider it an experience, and understand that you'll feel amazingly more confident with similar encounters in the future. There will always be compensation to you, no matter what the outcome. You'll always win, either by accidentally coming off just like you wanted, or by gaining experience that will make you ever so much more suave and cool in future encounters. So, relax. Either way, you can't lose.

4 *Talk with Confidence*

Wouldn't you like to be able to talk to the one you want with confidence? Then it's important that you are accepting of yourself. Don't inhibit your efforts to converse with others because you fear what they might think of you. What you say is not nearly as important as the fact that you say *something* to at least get the ball rolling. As you become accustomed to speaking in spite of your fears, your conversational ability will improve.

STARTING A CONVERSATION

What is the best way to start a conversation with someone new? People are more uncomfortable with this aspect of social interaction than any other. There is pressure on the person who is trying to initiate the conversation, as well as on the one being approached. A few key techniques can put everyone at ease. Starting a conversation need not be that difficult. In fact, once you get over your initial reluctance, you'll find making conversation an effective instrument to help you win the one you want.

You must first realize that conversation involves more than words. It also includes eye contact and, to some extent, body language. Realize, too, that facial expressions are a crucial part of the conversation process. If you do your best to continue smiling even as you stumble over your words, you are assured to make a good impression.

CONVERSATION ANXIETIES

Now let's get down to basics. One of the main reasons people feel uncomfortable starting a conversation with someone new is the fear of rejection. You, too, may worry about this. How humiliating. How shameful. Can't you just picture yourself slinking off in embarrassment? Dispel such thoughts! The key to successful conversation isn't the use of fancy words in an attempt to make a good impression. The secret is to come across as *warm* and *caring* And as long as you are making a sincere effort to communicate, that's exactly how you'll come across. If you're sincere, you'll never make a bad impression. It's when you *try* to be impressive that you get into trouble.

What to Say

Is there anything you can say to get the conversation ball rolling? Yes, just about anything. Even hackneyed phrases that indicate you've been watching old movies will do. You might feel funny walking up to somebody you've never met and saying something trite like, "Excuse me, but you look *so* familiar. Haven't I seen you somewhere before?" but such an effort can work. It's part of human nature to be flattered by attention, and the people you approach in this fashion will eat it up—more often than you may think!

Small Talk

Making small talk is a common way to break the ice when meeting new people. This is because such talk focuses on subjects that are non-threatening and impersonal, such as the weather, the surrounding location, or other people. The advantage of small talk is that it gives people the chance to warm up to you a bit and learn to trust you *before* making themselves vulnerable to you. A slow, gentle approach is better than coming on like gangbusters! Of course, small talk alone won't get you very far in developing a deep relationship. It merely serves as a temporary transition to more meaningful conversation.

"Bigger" Talk

As soon as it's appropriate, personalize the conversation. Begin to discuss feelings and attitudes that are normally missing in small talk. Once you have gotten the ball rolling, gradually ask questions that show an interest in the other person. Ask about that person's experiences. Mention something about yourself occasionally, but do so only as it relates to the other person (to show you can identify with what he or she is saying). Then quickly return the spotlight. If he or she asks you some questions about yourself, answer without getting carried away. Remember that interest has its limits! Especially in the early stages of conversation, reveal only enough about yourself to whet the other's appetite for wanting to know more! Always maintain some mystery about yourself—it will keep people coming back. Think of your conversations as a great banquet in which the other person is the main course and you are the seasoning. Don't overdo it. You don't want the main course to be too spicy!

Of course, it's important to mention that you must avoid even the *appearance* of bragging. Nothing is a bigger turnoff than people who seems to get "high" on recounting endless facts about themselves. Another no-no involves speaking negatively of others. Unfortunately, some people like to make conversation by putting others down in some way. Uniting themselves with anyone who will join them in such backstabbing ventures gives them a false sense of acceptance. But don't fall into this trap! All it does is sow seeds of distrust in the people you meet. If you would put down one person, how can others be sure you won't do the same thing to them? They can't. So avoid this and any other form of negative backbiting. It will leave a bad impression on the one you want. It's better to speak positively and supportingly of others. As the saying goes, "If you can't say somethin' nice, don't say nothin' at all!"

Conversation Summary

In conclusion, realize that *you* must accept the responsibility for initiating and maintaining successful conversation if you hope to win the one you want. You can't leave such a vital element of a developing relationship to chance. You must be in control. This doesn't mean you should do most of the talking; rather, you should maintain successful conversation largely by listening and asking questions. Your main goal is simply to communicate to the person that you care. Encourage that person to do most of the talking; just make sure you have plenty of fuel to feed the fire when the flame looks like it's dying out. A little planning can help. Have some ideas in mind ahead of time. Think of topics you can bring up to spark conversation. Many years ago, a person we know was quite nervous about an upcoming date and wondered how he could keep the conversation flowing comfortably. He finally resorted to writing down a list of possible topics on a 3-x-5 index card, which he discreetly referred to throughout the evening. It worked great!

Try not to get too hung up on the particulars. Just remember to be warm and caring. Even if you're not totally confident with your conversational abilities, you can show that you care by being a good listener. Others like that. Remember—people don't care how much you *know* until they know how much you *care!*

5 *Know What You Want in a Prospective Mate*

Before going on to the rest of the love tactics in this book, you should have a clear idea of the characteristics and qualities you're looking for in the one you want. At times, the going may get quite tough, and being sure that the one you want is the one you *really* want will be the only source of strength and motivation you may have to fall back on. With clearly defined goals, you'll be more committed to following through and doing what is necessary to win that person over.

Some people don't even realize that they are attracted to others because of certain qualities. They've never analyzed their reasons for becoming enamored in the first place. For them, love remains a mystery. They are like lost ships in the midst of an ocean without maps to guide them, drifting aimlessly without control over their own destiny. But you must be different! For those who understand the forces that guide them and know where they want to go, it is possible to chart their own course. And that's exactly what we expect you to do.

First, make a list of all the people you can remember being attracted to or having crushes on during your life. Then, next to each name, write down all the things you remember liking about that person. What exactly was it that you found attractive? Was it their smile? Their eyes? The way they laughed? Think of their characters. Were they kind? Self-assured? Intelligent? Did they have a good sense of humor? Review this list and then ask yourself what other qualities you would like the person of your dreams to have. Soon you will come up with a pretty good profile of your ideal person. Now don't panic just because you don't think such a person exists. This is just a starting point.

Knowing what characteristics you'd like in a person will better prepare you to begin your search. This doesn't mean, however, that your expectations will remain inflexible. You'll be surprised at how easy it will be to adjust your wants according to the real live prospects that are available. Consider this list a frame of reference for starting out. Obviously, you may revise your list if you like. Furthermore, you may discover that you are still attracted to many people who don't meet all of your ideal expectations. But simply knowing what that ideal is will help give you power in your search.

6 *Plan Out Where to Meet Others*

As much help as the love tactics in this book can be once you have actually found someone you want, it wouldn't be complete without some suggestions as to *where* you may find a prospective mate. This section will briefly discuss a few settings to possibly plant a few romantic seeds.

ON THE JOB

The workplace is typically one of the very best sources for meeting people. First of all, there is opportunity. Most people spend a lot of time at work, where they can become acquainted with customers, clients, and co-workers. Second, the distraction of the work environment provides a casual atmosphere for becoming acquainted. Typically, daily activities at work are focused around other business, which takes away some of the pressure often inherent in trying to get to know someone better.

Countless couples have met through work-related circumstances. Although some people feel it is risky to become romantically involved with people at work, others believe it is worth the risk. Only you can decide if the gamble is worth it in your particular situation.

SPECIAL INTEREST GROUPS

Another gold mine for potential romance lies in clubs or special interest groups. For starters, health and fitness clubs, book clubs, swim and/or ski clubs probably exist near your home. Furthermore, you can always take a class. Pick up a catalogue from a community adult-education program or a local college that offers continuing education courses, and browse through it for topics of interest. The classroom is probably the best place to become acquainted with members of the opposite sex.

Service organizations also provide a fertile field for seeds of introduction to grow and flourish. When you work side by side with someone for a charitable cause, it makes relationship development as easy as 1-2-3. And don't discount the possibility of meeting someone at your place of worship. Many single people who attend church or synagogue tend to think in terms of permanence, and have goals like marriage and family. They are more likely to want to settle down and less likely to be thrilled with the idea of one-night stands. One young man told us he believed the best place to meet women was in church. He reported that his most stable and enjoyable relationships began there. (As an added bonus, the girls' parents often invited him for Sunday dinner!)

Don't assume that you need special skills or must meet rigid requirements to get involved in any of these groups or associations. A simple phone call asking for information and expressing an interest in getting involved is usually all it takes. Most people will be happy to help you out.

REFERRALS THROUGH FRIENDS

No matter how you decide to improve your social circulation, there is one method you must not overlook. Rely on your existing network of friends. This is often one of the safest ways to proceed, even though you may not know ahead of time who you're going to be "fixed up" with. But because friends are screening your potential dates, you can feel fairly confident in their choices.

One young guy we know named James had a creative way of meeting people with the help of a married couple he knew. He had the couple bring one of their single female friends to concerts or sports events. Unknown to the girl, James would occupy the fourth seat, and meet her "unexpectedly." As this appeared to be a "chance" meeting between James and the couple's friend, the pressure was off, and it was easy for them to get to know each other.

THE SINGLES SCENE

The problem with most bars and clubs is that they are largely associated with temporary dalliances. Many people refuse to go to bars because they consider them "pickup joints" where the best they can hope for is a one-night stand. Deep down, most single people are really looking for a lasting, permanent relationship. People don't want to settle for table scraps when they could be feasting at the banquet of true love.

Unlike bars, which are devoted primarily to drinking, most dances that are open to the public don't have the same negative reputation. Some, however, find it difficult to meet people at dances because they first have to break the ice. On the other hand, once this fear is overcome, many people find this an especially effective and enjoyable way to spend their time.

Dating services and singles clubs can be another successful way to meet people. However, before joining or getting involved with such groups or services, it's a good idea to do a little research to be sure they're reputable. Singles groups that are affiliated with religious organizations or community centers are usually good bets, but if there is a profit involved with the organization, be careful. Also, be wary of small, privately advertised groups or services that don't have any known affiliations. It's always best if you know members of a club before joining.

Personal ads in newspapers and magazines are commonly used to make romantic connections. Although this was once considered a sleazy approach, today, respectable people from every profession and age group take out these ads, often with a great deal of success. If you decide to take out a personal ad, be sure to place it in a reputable publication. It's also a good idea to review existing ads to get an idea of what to say.

MEETING ONLINE

Probably the greatest opportunity for meeting people has come about with the arrival of the computer age and access to the Internet. Online opportunities for making connections are virtually limitless. Everyone—even those who are most timid—can take positive steps toward meeting others with the simple click of a mouse. Although it is unlikely that you can win someone's heart without an eventual "in-person" meeting, the Internet will at least provide you the initial opportunity to meet people. Communicating online provides a comfortable, anonymous setting through which you are afforded the opportunities to practice some of your love tactics. And with such unlimited opportunities, you can improve your skills at a slow, comfortable pace and without pressure.

In the movie *Groundhog Day,* smug TV weatherman Phil Connors goes to Punxsutawney, Pennsylvania, to cover the traditional Groundhog Day ceremonies. Rude and egocentric, Connors goes through the day, only to discover that he is trapped in time, condemned to replay the same day over and over—that is, until he finally learns to live that day as a decent human being. At first, he was completely frustrated at the daily challenges he continued to endure; but eventually, he began changing his negative behavior. The message? Practice makes perfect.

In the same way, most romantic-type mistakes are due simply to inexperience. Practice will help eradicate most of these errors over time, making one a true "artist" in the skill of romance. If you are determined to learn, the Internet can provide the necessary experience—endless opportunities for interacting with others. And if your attempt to develop an online relationship seems to stall, no problem, there are always countless other relationships for you to pursue.

Keep in mind, though, that any online interactions are just preludes to face-to-face meetings. Ideally, the Internet can serve as a vehicle to help you *initiate* prospective long-term relationships. Ultimately, however, it is up to you to cultivate a more committed relationship through personal, face-to-face interactions with the one you want.

The ABCs of Developing Internet Prospects

Once you begin meeting people online who are interested in further developing a relationship with you, proceed thoughtfully. The following guidelines are designed to assist.

1. **E-mail.** Begin the communication with another person through the exchange of e-mail. Responding to these "electronic" letters at your leisure, gives you lots of time to think about your responses.

2. **Online chats.** Once you feel the relationship has developed into one that is mutually profitable and enjoyable, you might consider moving to an online chat room, where you can engage in "live" conversations with that person. You can also carry on a live chat if you and the other party both have "Instant Message" capabilities on your computers. Initially, try to keep these conversations limited from a few minutes to a half hour. Eventually, they can extend into conversations that go on for longer periods.

3. **Phone conversations.** Once you feel comfortable with the online relationship, direct voice communication by telephone is the next step.

4. **Face-to-face meetings.** Finally, after having successful phone conversations, the next step in a developing relationship is an in-person meeting—also known as the "big date."

One thing to keep in mind through this whole process is that all of these steps are merely *tools* for meeting new prospects. Part of becoming good at love tactics is through practicing the principles. The real value of the Internet lies in its capability to provide unlimited opportunities for getting this practice through meeting potential mates. But remember, you cannot truly win another person's heart until face-to-face encounters actually begin.

Never be discouraged just because you don't seem to be getting the best results right away. Even Casanova had to practice his skills of love before he became good at them. Just realize that the behavior principles and love tactics presented in this book are your tools, and with experience, you will gain the skills to use them effectively. Practice makes perfect. The more you practice the love tactics, the more effective you will become at applying them. Eventually, you will be able to apply them with perfect skill and confidence. You will become a "master" of love.

Be realistic. Don't expect to get a date with every person you meet on the Internet. Figure that for every five satisfactory e-mail or e-chat relationships, just one may advance to a phone relationship. And for every five phone relationships, only one may advance to a date.

We know a number of happily married couples who have met online. And we recommend this method of communication as a valuable option for finding the one you want.

A WORD (OR TWO) TO THE SHY

We are aware that some of you reading this book may have a very difficult time getting started because of shyness. This is nothing to be ashamed of! In fact, being shy is actually quite common. Many people (more than you realize) are so afraid of encountering others that they keep themselves shut up at home constantly. If you fall into the shyness category, we understand your dilemma, but you mustn't let it hold you back from winning the one you want. If you are having a hard time getting started, we'd like to offer a few suggestions.

First, remember that actually doing the thing you fear is the best way to deflate that fear. Practice will help you become more confident. Try the Internet. The nice thing about interacting with people online is that you can practice your conversational skills within a very safe and secure environment. You don't have to move up to a more direct form of interaction until you are ready.

SOME FINAL THOUGHTS

Eventually, you'll be ready for dates. However, if you still find it hard to approach someone directly, having a friend set you up on a blind date may be a good idea. Don't be afraid to do this. Why? It's practice, and the more practice you have, the more self-assured you'll become. Go for the blind dates. Eventually, you'll feel confident enough to make dates on your own.

Consider the great Greek orator Demosthenes, who, initially, was very unsure of himself, and very uncomfortable with his speaking skills. He used to practice talking when he was alone at the beach by putting pebbles in his mouth and then trying to speak clearly above the sound of the breaking waves. With persistence and desire you, too, will improve your communication skills and gain supreme self-confidence!

If you are shy, you can still win the one you want. You may have to take small steps in the beginning, but those small steps will help accomplish your goal as long as you keep on practicing. "If at first you don't succeed, try, try, again!" Good luck and happy hunting!

3

Taking the Offensive

Principle: *People are like mirrors, always reflecting the same attitudes that they think others have towards them.*

---

*T*he one you want is out there waiting for someone to love. The miracle is that you can be that someone! All you have to do is take the initiative to act. Human beings are designed to return those feelings of love that they recognize as genuine. Your first challenge is to look into your own heart and make sure your love *is* real, and then, second, effectively communicate that love. Both responsibilities require you to take control of the situation from the very beginning and not leave anything to fate.

At times, it may seem easier to sit back and blame romantic set-backs on your incompatible astrological signs (". . . by the way, what's *your* sign?"), but the real problem is your own inaction. As Shakespeare so wisely put it, "The fault, dear Brutus, is not in our stars, but in ourselves." You, alone, hold the key to your success. You must be determined to turn that key, especially in this most vital challenge of your life.

As the authors of this book, we can reveal the secrets of *what* to do, but only you can actually do it. Even at this early stage of the book, adopt the motto, "If it's to be, it's up to me!"

♥ 7 *Be First to Show Interest in the Other*

One of the most helpful facts about human nature is that we most often take notice of and feel attracted to people who appear to have a genuine interest *in us.* It's what makes your heart skip a beat when you catch someone looking at you across a crowded room. All of us are susceptible to such kinds of attention. Surprisingly, the best way to favorably impress others is *not* by telling them marvelous things about you, but by letting them know that you are favorably impressed *by them.*

People are reflective creatures, similar to mirrors. Many of our attitudes and behaviors toward others are greatly determined by the way others treat us first. So the way we feel about others is generally a reflection of the way we think others feel about us. For example, who do you usually smile at? Those who smile at you first, of course! Also, don't you tend to dislike people who you suspect may secretly (or not so secretly) dislike you? The most important revelation of all, however, is that you love those who you truly believe love you!

The secret, then, to winning someone's love is to first convince that person of your real, genuine love. If you want to succeed at love, you must *act*, not *react!* You want love to flow *from* you, and not merely be reflected *by* you! This requires patience and self-mastery, which are the ultimate keys to winning the one you want.

Too often we sit back and wait for "Mr. or Ms. Right" to come along and show us how much they care before we are willing to commit ourselves to care back. But there's something we should realize. Everybody else does the same thing! Nobody (or very few people, anyway) wants to be the one to take the lead because of the pain and effort that must be invested.

If you're simply waiting around for your dream person to show up, you could have a very long wait. Don't leave your love life to fate. Take advantage of your opportunities! There's a whole world of people out there waiting for you to sweep them off their feet. All you need is the courage to take the first step.

Showing interest in the other person *first* means being the first to smile, make eye contact, extend a vocal greeting, spark a conversation, and suggest getting together. *Don't give up, even if there is no immediate response.*

Taking a visible interest in the other person is the first step to winning his or her heart. It immediately fills that person's need for attention (and *everyone* needs attention!). It also paves the way for the future, but doesn't insure a positive response right away. That will come in time. Meanwhile, continue to show interest as you develop your skills in the more advanced techniques.

Go for One Date at a Time

Q: How do you eat an elephant?
A: One bite at a time.
Q: How do you win someone's heart?
A: One *date* at a time.

As soon as you have gained someone's attention, it's time to begin building a relationship. This is done by spending exclusive blocks of time together, commonly known as "dates." A date is simply an opportunity to interact with the one you want on a personal level—one on one.

The first date can be very uncomfortable for both parties. This is because it is a journey into the unknown—neither party knows what to expect. It is a time for getting to know the other person and learning about his or her likes, dislikes, and idiosyncrasies. This can make the first date very interesting. Be yourself, but don't start revealing your faults and self-doubts. We all have them, of course, but you want the other person to leave with a warm feeling of having spent an enjoyable evening with someone who is confident.

Something magical happens when people spend time together. They grow on each other. There is a psychologically binding effect. Magnetic forces between people are a very real psychological phenomenon. However, don't prematurely expose your anxiousness by trying to tie up the social calendar of the one you want. Suggesting more than one date at a time can be dangerous to your hopes. It is likely to frighten off a potential sweetheart before the binding effect has even begun. At the same time, don't settle for less than a real date. Don't believe that a relationship can grow just by seeing someone every day at class or at work. This type of interaction won't provide enough romantic electricity to adequately charge the relationship.

So set your sights on getting that first date. Work for it until you succeed. Then, after having the date and giving it a little time to be digested emotionally, go for another one. Don't push for too much commitment at once. By focusing on one date at a time, you'll actually be building the relationship, but at a rate that is slow enough to keep from chasing away the one you want.

There is a story recounted about an Arab sheik who was making a journey to a distant city. In order to get there, he had to travel through an extensive desert. While on his way, there was a terrible windstorm that forced the sheik to set up a small tent for shelter. The wind was furious and the sand beat wildly on the outside of the tent, but he was safe and snug within. Suddenly, from outside, he heard the pleading voice of his camel.

"Oh please, kind master," the camel asked, "the wind is so harsh and the beating sand so unrelenting. May I please shelter just my mouth and nose from the storm by placing them in the safety of the tent through the tent door?"

The sheik, touched by the humble nature of his faithful camel's request, thought, "Surely my faithful servant, who carries me so tirelessly and without complaint through scorching desert, deserves some respite from these savage winds." So he permitted the camel to put his nose and mouth just inside the tent door.

After a while, the camel said, "Oh kind master, thank you for the relief you have afforded me by your goodness and mercy. Is it possible that I might also shelter my eyes from the stinging sands?" To make a long story short, the sheik eventually found himself on the outside of the tent in the middle of the violent sandstorm, wondering how he had somehow changed places with the camel. The answer: The camel kept his requests for favors so simple and humble that the sheik couldn't refuse him. The smaller the request, the harder it is to deny!

It is the same when developing a relationship. You must spend time with the person *one on one* to build it properly. This requires many dates, but ask for only one date at a time. Furthermore, if the one you want seems hesitant to grant you time even for a single date, be creative. Think of something you can ask the person to do with you, even if it involves just a few minutes. Perhaps you can ask the person to join you for a quick hamburger or an ice cream cone, with the promise that you'll have them back home before they know it! Who could be so cold-hearted as to refuse such a humble request? Little by little, you'll surely reach your goal.

WHO ASKS WHOM?

A common mistake many people make is to try to get the other person to ask *them* out. Take the story of a couple we'll call Kathleen and Larry. When Kathleen met Larry—the new guy at work—he really "rang her chimes" like nobody before, and quickly became the one she wanted. She tried to make it obvious that she was interested in him. Although Larry was very nice to her at work, he never asked her out socially.

Kathleen correctly understood that in order for the relationship to progress, they *had* to go out together. However, she mistakenly concluded that the only way to accomplish this was to somehow entice Larry into asking her out. She wrote him a note saying that she had come to appreciate his friendship and wanted to get to know him better. She hoped this letter would encourage Larry to take the first step and ask her out, but he never even acknowledged her note.

The lesson here is to take responsibility for furthering the relationship by doing the asking. Trying to shift this responsibility to the other party is *not* the way to succeed. In this case, Larry never even mentioned receiving Kathleen's note, so she wound up feeling worse than she did before sending it.

TAKING THE FIRST STEP . . .

Developing a relationship is like learning to walk. Focus *only* on that first step. If you try to get too far ahead of yourself, you'll trip and fall. Of course, even when you're just concentrating on that first step (the first date), things can still prove to be elusive. It doesn't matter. Don't be deterred! You won't get anywhere without the first step. So just make up your mind that you'll work for that first date until you get it. Anyone with a fair amount of dating experience will tell you that things don't always fall into place. Even the most attractive and popular people encounter obstacles in their dating efforts. Did you know that John F. Kennedy was once rebuffed by Sophia Loren? So try not to take it personally if things don't work out initially. As the song goes, "Just pick yourself up, dust yourself off, and start all over again."

BE LIKE IKE

Former President Dwight D. Eisenhower experienced the same frustration when trying to get a date with the one he wanted back in his single days. His dream girl told him she was booked up, not only for the following weekend, but also for the next three weekends! Now the average guy might have taken the hint and given up. But Dwight wasn't your average guy, and he chose to *act* rather than *react!* He was determined to get that first date and waited until Mamie finally said "yes" for the fourth weekend. The rest is history.

STEP BY STEP

Remember that even though the first date may not be easy to get, sometimes it *does* come easily, and it may be the follow-up date that's hard to get. Or they may *both* prove elusive. Or . . . whatever! Just keep in mind that the most important date for you to concentrate on getting is the *next one!* Eventually, if you keep concentrating on moving one step at a time (while appropriately applying the tactics in this book), resistance will melt, and the one you want will finally become like putty in your hands! The beginning of any project is always the hardest. A wise man once said, "That which we persist in doing becomes easier. Not that the nature of the thing has changed, but our ability to achieve has increased."

9 ♥ *Avoid Being Defensive*

The most difficult part of being the first person to extend yourself in a relationship and show interest in the other is that it leaves you extremely vulnerable. If the one you want shows no indication of reciprocating your friendship, it may leave you feeling foolish.

When this happens, your natural first impulse may be to take quick defensive action, as you immediately try to cover up your foolishness and redeem your pride. How do you do this? Generally, by withdrawing from the contest or, even worse, trying to take some punitive action toward the one who has rejected you. For example, you might bitterly snub the person or speak badly of them to others. This kind of defensive behavior, however, generally backfires and makes the situation worse. What many people never realize is that rejection can almost always be overcome through patience and endurance. This is best accomplished by continuing to meet your prospective loved one's basic needs for attention, understanding, acceptance, appreciation, and affection even though he or she may be neglecting yours. It takes patience and fortitude to be a true and unconditional friend to others, but it pays off in the end.

British politician Lord Melbourne once said, "Neither man nor woman can be worth anything until they have discovered they are fools . . . (and) the sooner the discovery is made the better, as there is more time and power for taking advantage of it." So don't be afraid to look foolish. This fear only paralyzes your ability to reach out to others. And it is only by reaching out consistently that you can maximize the level of trust others will feel for you. Furthermore, there is no shame in rejection. Endure it well. All great human beings have gone through it.

Allowing yourself to remain open and vulnerable to another human being, even in the face of rejection and at the risk of feeling foolish, shows sincerity and character. It will persuade others to become similarly open with you. On the other hand, becoming defensive when someone hurts you by not responding to your attention is certainly not the answer. It only reinforces the person's distant attitude and justification in his or her initial standoffishness towards you. By exhibiting a sort of "If-you-don't-want-me-then-I-don't-want-you" type of attitude, you demonstrate very clearly that your ability to be a true friend is shallow. Deep down, people sense their need for someone with staying power, someone who will stick with them in spite of themselves, and love them even when they act unlovable.

So if the other person is resisting, you have a better chance of defusing that resistance with behavior that is *not defensive*. Don't fight fire with fire—you might wind up burning down the whole house! Drown the fires of resistance with waters of acceptance and love. "Love is surrender" are the words of a popular song, but what these words are *really* saying is that sincere caring can be conveyed only after one has surrendered his or her ego and false pride. Make the effort to achieve unconditional friendship and stick with it, even if the going gets tough. Don't get defensive just because the sincerity of the love you extend doesn't seem to sufficiently impress itself upon someone's heart when you first offer it.

RECOVERING FROM REJECTION

No matter who you are, you're going to experience some degree of rejection in trying to win someone's heart. If not in the very beginning, then at some point down the road. Try not to let this shake you. For heaven's sake, don't resort to negative reactions towards the one you want when you experience this. It might comfort your wounded ego a bit to strike out, but it'll also cost you a good opportunity to build a successful relationship. Great victories in romance are always accompanied by a little pain along the way. No pain, no gain. No war was ever won without losing a few battles first, so you mustn't give up the fight just because today's struggle seemed to end in defeat. Remember that you're not beat until you quit! And, friend, we've got news for you: You're just getting started!

As we've said, people are like mirrors. Eventually, whatever attitudes you send out will come home again. Putting up defensive barriers will encourage others to maintain them as well. Instead, counter their apathetic responses with renewed love, kindness, and attention. Continue to be positive even if they react negatively, and return good for evil as the Bible advises. Let down your defensive barriers. Don't provide others with any ammunition to justify keeping theirs up, and in time you'll find them letting theirs down, too! As psychoanalyst Erich Fromm so aptly observed, falling in love is actually just "the sudden collapse of barriers" between two people.

Allowing yourself to become vulnerable to another human being shows that you care more about the *person* than the *reaction* he or she may have for you. Over an extended period of time, this non-defensive approach is guaranteed to produce positive changes in that person's observable behavior towards you.

4

Making Time an Ally

Principle: *The more time a relationship between two people has to grow and mature, the stronger the bonds of emotional attachment will be.*

---

uthor James Thurber once said, "Love is what you've been through with somebody." Reflection on this statement will bring nods of agreement from any thoughtful human being. Of course, we love those with whom we have shared life itself. And the more of life we've shared, the deeper the love. Take, for example, the great emotional bonds that exist between the remaining members of a battle-seasoned war battalion. What exactly causes these people—whose personalities and temperaments are so diverse—to join together? It is *shared experience*—the good and the bad. The more experiences people have gone through together, the stronger the bond! Ask anyone who has lost a spouse after many years of marriage. They'll be able to fill you in.

Day by day, little by little, the threads of experience that people share are like strands of a spider's web that carefully bind them ever more closely to each other. The bonding process is so subtle that most people don't even realize they have become emotionally "stuck" on each other until they attempt to sever the relationship. Their success in walking away free and clear at that time depends a great deal upon how much experience has been shared between them. And, of course, *that* depends upon how much time has been allowed for the experience to occur. The more time the relationship has had a chance to grow, generally speaking, the stronger it will be—and the more painful it will be to separate. It was George Washington who said, "Friendship is a plant of *slow* growth."

10 *Take Your Time (Go Slowly)*

Most marriage experts agree that, on average, the strongest marriages appear to be those in which the couples have taken at least a year to get to know each other before tying the knot. Consider the example of Theodore Roosevelt, who was known for his enthusiastic nature, and yet took a year and a half to develop a good, strong relationship with his sweetheart, Alice Hathaway Lee, before they got married. He openly acknowledged that his adoration of her knew no limits. Roosevelt's strong feelings were probably intensified by the fact that Alice held him at bay—practically at arm's length—throughout their entire blossoming relationship!

Had his sweetheart been too eager to express a willingness to commit herself to him, either by spoken word or through physical affection, Roosevelt's passionate desire for her certainly would not have been as great. The very fact that his state of anticipated desire was sustained for so long is what provided the foundation for his subsequent lifelong adoration for her. Although Alice eventually "broke down" and fell for him, ironically, it was probably his initial anxiousness that kept her from total commitment. Roosevelt understood the frustration of taking it slow in winning the one he wanted. Almost from the moment he met Alice, he knew she was the girl for him. He vowed in the privacy of his journal "that win her I would, if it were possible." Still, their relationship took a year and a half before she returned his affection.

Have you ever tried to rush a budding romance along too quickly? This is a very common mistake. Since relationships grow stronger with the passing of time, the trick in succeeding is to keep the friendship developing as long as possible without frightening off a potential lover. Unfortunately, what most of us do instead is try to extract some sort of commitment from the one we want at the earliest possible moment. This can seem threatening and ominous. Why? It makes people feel as if they're being forced into something before they're ready—like they're being backed into a corner, which makes them anxious to find an escape. If people are allowed to progress at their own pace, however, the natural course of their emotional growth will lead them to actually feel comfortable about making such a commitment.

Compare winning the one you want with going fishing. When you throw your hook into the water and feel that first nibble, you can't jerk the line too quickly. Sure, it's a temptation to pull on the line and reel that fish in right away, but if you act *too* quickly, you'll wind up pulling the hook right out of the fish's mouth, losing it completely! The hook needs time to work itself into the mouth and become securely imbedded. Given enough time, the fish will do most of the work for you, as long as you supply the hook and the bait. So give your lure enough time to work its magic in love, as well. Your human "fish" will bite the bait, just make sure you give it time to become firmly attached to your hook! Do you see the analogy? Make sure the relationship is good and strong before you begin to "reel in" your sweetheart.

FEAR OF COMMITMENTS

Why do people resist getting involved in relationships? Is it love they are running from? Actually, no. People run from making commitments, *not* from being loved! It's only when they start to feel obligated by accepting another's love that they'll turn away. And when we hint that we're including someone in our future plans, that person's natural instinct is to run away fast and as far away as possible!

We learned the story of one man who led a life of fraud. He used a number of aliases in his scams as he traveled around the country. During one particular journey, he met a woman, and although he deceived her initially, he soon realized he felt differently about her.

He found himself falling in love and felt a strong desire to marry her and "go straight." Although this would have meant completely changing his deceitful lifestyle, there was no doubt in his mind that this was what he wanted.

When he asked the woman to marry him, he also confessed to her about his past. She was so shocked, she called the police! He had no choice but to quickly hop on a plane and get away. Although he didn't have much time to mourn his loss as he was making his escape, a few hours later he became introspective. Only a short time earlier, he had wanted to marry this woman more than he had ever wanted anything in his entire life, but now he had to face the fact that there was no chance of that ever happening. He felt something emotionally, but couldn't identify the feeling. It wasn't really disappointment. It wasn't anger. Then it dawned on him—it was *relief.* In spite of the fact that he *had* wanted to marry this woman, he was also relieved that he didn't have to! Forces beyond his control had freed him of any feelings of emotional attachment or obligation. He felt a new appreciation and, indeed, exhilaration for his newfound sense of freedom.

The truth is, *it's common to feel two conflicting desires at the same time.* One is usually just a little stronger than the other, so that's the one we're most aware of. On one hand, we desire to be free and uncommitted; on the other hand, we yearn to belong to someone. So, while trying to win someone's heart, *don't ignore their ever-present desire to remain free* (even though at times it may be hidden from view). This underscores the wisdom of going slowly. You don't want to scare that person off before he or she is ready for a commitment!

So how do you succeed at this? By taking your time. Don't rush to reveal your anxiousness to be with that person all of the time. Let him or her think that you have only limited intentions of getting together again in the future—possibly one date, but nothing more. And if that person doesn't agree to that one date, back off completely for a while before trying again. This is called "keeping from getting too serious." It doesn't mean that you should stop paying attention to the person forever. It just means that you should keep your long-range intentions to yourself.

Everyone has a personal need for emotional breathing space. If you want someone to be comfortable seeing you, you can't threaten his or her freedom. Don't give anyone reason to believe that you are expecting them to share their life and future with you. Otherwise, like someone who is choking and fighting for air, that person may desperately seek to escape from you.

As long as you keep a person believing that the relationship is merely casual, time will be on your side. Meanwhile, the subconscious process of emotional bonding will continue to bind that person's heart more closely to yours.

Don't Panic

Let's say you're trying to do the right thing. You're taking your time in developing the relationship before introducing the element of passion, but then, unexpectedly, someone else starts moving in on your guy or girl! This new competition is likely to make you feel pressured. It's natural to feel that if you don't get moving and "sew this one up" for yourself right away, you might lose that person permanently.

Don't panic! Remember Aesop's fable about the race between the tortoise and the hare? The hare, with its great speed, seemed to be a shoo-in as the winner. However, the tortoise continued plodding along, never giving up and never deviating from the proper course. There must have been moments during the race when the tortoise thought, "Why bother?" since his rival had the obvious advantage. But in the end, his determination and "slow-but-steady" method turned out to be the best. People often spend years unwittingly sabotaging one relationship after another by rushing romance.

Haste Invariably Makes Waste

What if rivals do come on the scene and start a relationship with the one you want? And what if they try to quickly introduce romance into that relationship? Although they may appear to be successful at first, they themselves are likely to be moving too fast, and this will create a flaw in the foundation of their relationship. We've seen this happen time and time again. A fast romance can be compared to a shooting star that burns brightly, but doesn't last. The actions of a rival can actually work to your advantage if, like the tortoise in Aesop's fable, you keep building your own relationship in an unhurried and meaningful way.

Your competitors will experience obstacles—they always do. And when that happens, they'll pay the price for not taking sufficient time to build a good solid foundation of pure friendship first. By then, you'll be ready to step in and take over! When the one you want is feeling the need for someone who really cares about and loves them unconditionally, you'll be ready to pick up the pieces and carry that person across the finish line! You'll have your romance, too. But it will occur at the proper time—later—and it will be all the more powerful for your having waited!

11 Be Attentive on a Regular Basis

In *The Little Prince*, by Antoine de Saint-Exupéry, the importance of showing regular, almost clock-regulated, attention to someone you'd like to win is clearly demonstrated. In this classic allegorical commentary on love, a lonely but skeptical fox meets a little prince who is out "looking for friends." The fox realizes that he, too, would like a friend, but he is also very aware of his own instinctive nature to run away at the first hint of being pursued. He pleads with the little prince to undertake the challenging task of taming him, but the prince doesn't know how to accomplish such a feat. He asks the fox how to do so.

The fox, although bound to obey his instincts, also has a clear understanding of how to get around them. So first, he tells the prince to expect to exercise great patience in this process. He instructs the prince to sit a distance from him in a field of grass, just to observe him for a while. (The fox knows this will gratify his own need for attention without threatening his sense of freedom.)

Admitting his own apprehensions, the fox warns the little prince that even though it may not appear obvious, he will actually be very aware of the prince's presence, ever watching him out of the corner of his eye. However, he further explains that as long as the prince doesn't make any sudden, quick movements in his effort to tame him, and as long as sits a little closer to the fox each day, the time will come when a relationship will begin to develop. The fox adds that if the prince comes at the same time each day, the pleasure of his anticipation will be enhanced as the appointed hour draws nigh.

How does this apply to you? In your efforts to "tame" the one you want and win his or her heart, *show attention on a regular basis.* Just as the little prince conditioned the fox to expect his attentions at regular intervals, you can subconsciously program the one you want to perceive you as a part of his or her life. Condition that person to expect your presence regularly, even though, initially, it may be viewed with some suspicion. If you don't make any rash or indiscreet efforts to "capture" the object of your affection, in time, that person will start becoming a bit curious about you and even begin to anticipate your appearances with some degree of subconscious gladness.

If you begin by making your presence felt in a person's life only once or twice a week, that's fine. But make sure you do so regularly enough that the person will notice if you don't show up. In time, people develop acceptance of anything that occurs with regularity.

Nothing is quite as powerful as the force of habit in influencing someone's behavior. But can a person actually become conditioned to feel *comfortable* in your presence? The answer is yes! The famous Russian scientist Ivan Pavlov did much to demonstrate the effects of conditioning on living creatures through his "salivating dog" experiments. After noticing that his dog would salivate a great deal more than usual when he was fed, he wondered if the dog could be programmed to produce the same reaction *without* the presence of food. So Pavlov rang a bell each time food was brought to the dog. With regularity, he continued pairing the dog's food with the sound of the bell. Eventually, the bell was rung without the food. Guess what. The dog salivated with the same anticipation as if it had just been presented with a juicy steak!

People can have similar "conditioned" experiences, sometimes without even realizing it. (This doesn't mean the one you want will

"salivate" at the mere thought of you. Although, you never know . . .)
If you show attention to another through regular telephone calls,
visits, and shared experiences, that person will subconsciously get
used to receiving regular attention from you. Where does this lead?
The person will become accustomed to feeling good when in your
presence, and subconsciously begin to look forward to your next
meeting.

12 Be Persistent

It's not easy to keep showing attention to someone who just seems to
want to brush you off. However, don't give up prematurely. Any act
of goodness or friendship extended towards another always makes
an impression, even if the results are not immediately noticeable.
Every action towards the one you want will bring you one step closer
to winning that person's heart.

One of Aesop's more famous stories involves a crow who was
dying of thirst. The bird came upon an abandoned pitcher that was
partially filled with water. The crow put his beak into the pitcher,
but found that he couldn't reach down far enough to get to the precious life-saving liquid. He seemed destined to die of dehydration,
even though, ironically, the water was only inches away. While in
this desperate circumstance, the crow suddenly had an idea. He
found a pebble and dropped it into the pitcher. Then he found another pebble, and dropped it into the pitcher as well. He continued
adding pebbles to the pitcher one at a time until the water was close
enough to reach.

Human beings have an unquenchable thirst for attention that
must be met constantly. Giving someone attention is like putting
pebbles into the pitcher of water. People are affected by it, whether or
not they appear to be. At first, you may not have any visible indication that the attention you are giving is accomplishing anything, but
be rest assured that it is! Keep trying. Whatever time and attention
you invest in a relationship will ultimately yield a most worthwhile
return. If you quit too soon, though, you may be depriving yourself
of love that may inevitably be yours!

DELAYED REACTION

Another reason persistence is so important is the *delayed-reaction effect*. Realize that you're trying to get the object of your affections to warm up to you. Often, the desired response will come, but not quickly enough to see the direct correlation between your action and the response.

Let's say, for example, that Jim has met Susan, who really strikes his fancy. He'd like to become much better acquainted with her. Imagine what might happen if, in one of their early encounters, Jim displayed a great deal of enthusiasm, as shown in the following scenario:

JIM: Hello, Susan! Remember me? We met at Jason Smith's party a couple weeks ago! What a surprise it is bumping into you here! Do you come here often? I'm here twice a week and don't remember ever seeing you in here before.

At this point, Jim is just trying to be friendly and strike up a conversation. Although he is a little nervous, he is trying to initiate some interaction. Even though Susan remembers Jim, she has never spoken with him at length. Caught off guard and taken back a little by his enthusiasm, Susan unintentionally comes across as standoffish and uninterested:

SUSAN: . . . er, hi. Uh, no, I don't usually come here . . .

She avoids looking Jim in the eye and instead appears to be looking around for somebody. Jim notices her lack of enthusiasm right away. He is aware that she isn't making eye contact with him and seems to be looking for an escape route. But he has already stepped into the situation, and feels he has to see it through. He tries to make the best of it with a warm smile and further attempts at conversation:

JIM: So have you seen Jason lately? I don't think I've talked to him since the night of that party where I met you. I wonder what he's been up to . . .

SUSAN: Uh . . . no, I haven't seen him either.

Then, without any attempt at prolonging the conversation:

SUSAN: Well, I'd better be running along . . .

It becomes apparent to Jim that his attempts are in vain. Obviously, Susan does not share his interest in becoming better friends (or so he thinks). He continues to smile and speak enthusiastically, but feels like a jerk:

JIM: Well, it's been real nice running into you! If you see Jason, tell him I said hi. Goodnight.

Susan feels relieved that this unexpected encounter is ending quickly enough. Actually, it's not that she dislikes Jim, she is simply not comfortable in knowing how to react to his enthusiasm, which has caught her off guard:

SUSAN: Uh, yeah . . . sure . . . Goodnight . . .

Afterwards, Jim thinks to himself, "Well, it's obvious enough she's not interested in getting to know me! I sure made a fool of myself on that one. Now it looks as though I like her, and she's just going to give me the cold shoulder. Well, I sure won't make *that* mistake again. I can tell when I'm not liked!"

Meanwhile, Susan has had a little time to emotionally process the encounter with Jim. To her surprise, she finds she even enjoyed it. "He was pretty nice," she thinks to herself after the fact. "And what a nice smile! I wonder if he could possibly be interested in me? Well, the next time the opportunity presents itself, I'm certainly going to try to get to know him better."

Susan's resolution, however, is already too late. Because she failed to respond to him initially, Jim has already decided to become more cool and distant—in other words, less vulnerable—in any future encounters with her.

The scenario continues as Jim and Susan meet again at the same place they had had their earlier encounter. Susan had gone there purposely, hoping for another "coincidental" meeting. She spots Jim and approaches him enthusiastically:

SUSAN: Hello Jim! What a coincidence bumping into you twice in one week! I guess it's fate, huh?

Jim, however, is determined not to play the fool:

JIM: Oh, hi. Fate? Yeah, guess so. Look, I've gotta run. See ya . . .

This time Jim goes away feeling a lot less foolish. And Susan is more convinced than ever that you cannot trust men. She thinks, "One day they act interested and the next, they couldn't care less about you!"

Perhaps Jim and Susan were both too hasty in their initial reactions, and allowed a potentially great relationship go down the tubes. There are a few lessons to be learned here. First, try not to be "overly" enthusiastic in your initial encounters with people. It may catch them off guard and result in unenthusiastic reactions. And second, don't abandon ship at the first sign of disinterest. Try to be determined and persistently friendly. Remember that when you plant a seed, often there is a delayed reaction effect. Have some faith in the tactics you're learning in this book. They'll work if you're willing to put them to the test. They won't let you down!

DON'T STALK

At this point, a word of caution is in order. When exercising persistence, you must be careful to recognize that there is a fine line between being persistent and being overbearing. Be careful not to cross that line. Remember, gaining respect from the one you want is of key importance when strategically following the love tactics in this book. And to do this, you must come across as cool, relaxed, and independent.

Trying to force a response from another person has several negative consequences. First, you may be viewed as desperate—a far cry from being independent, which is critical for winning respect and love. Second, you can get into serious legal trouble if you are accused of stalking.

Sometimes, inexperienced suitors *are* desperate because they simply don't know what to do or how to act. But even if you lack experience, it's crucial to understand the importance of being sensitive to another person's need for personal space. By demonstrating this intuitiveness and sensitivity, you are likely to actually gain stature in another's eyes. We have never heard of a case in which desperation and force did anything other than chase the other person away—and fast! But we do know of many instances in which patience and restraint have been victorious in winning another person's love.

It's only natural to panic and start pushing a little bit harder if you discover that the person you want is slipping away, especially if you feel that you were making progress with the relationship. But this, in fact, is the *very* time you should back away for a while. It will keep that person from locking his or her heart against you permanently, and keep the window of opportunity open for an appropriate time in the future. Don't ever feel as if you've lost the one you want just because you may have to retreat temporarily. Keep in mind that you are interested in winning the *war*, and that a tactical withdrawal from a losing battle can still be an integral part of that overall plan.

Persistence and patience go hand in hand. Force will backfire on you every time, even if it takes awhile to do so. Make time your ally, not your enemy. When it comes to building a relationship, progress at a slow, steady, persistent pace.

5

Pacifying Their Fears and Gaining Their Trust

Principle: *People have a subconscious need to remain free and emotionally uncommitted. Therefore, they will go to great lengths to avoid circumstances that threaten to limit that freedom.*

---

*I*t is extremely important to exercise restraint when sharing your hopes and dreams of a "future" with the one you want. There are some things you should keep to yourself, especially in the early stages of a relationship. Don't let the person think, particularly through verbal intimations, that your future happiness hinges on him or her. It will cause that individual to start feeling trapped. No one wants to be weighed down with such a responsibility. Many people will instinctively want "out" of the relationship before it goes any further.

On the other hand, if you are more discreet about your intentions, you have a better chance of keeping the relationship developing while the bonds of attachment grow ever stronger. It may seem silly to avoid talking about something that may appear obvious, but it is the least intimidating approach for *both* of you. People want to fall in love of their own volition; they don't want to be pushed. We agree with author Thomas Hardy's assessment that, "A lover without discretion is no lover at all." Blabbing blows everything. It's a sign of maturity to show restraint. By disclosing your intentions in the delicate early stages of romance, you may inadvertently drive the person away.

13 *Show You Care, But Don't Say It!*

Not long ago, a young woman named Roberta told us she was tired of all the "game playing" in her life as far as romantic relationships went. She claimed that all she wanted was someone who sincerely cared for her and who would lay his feelings on the line. She felt that she could respond emotionally to this kind of openness and candor, although we warned her that she would feel differently if it actually came to pass.

A few weeks after our conversation, a very eligible young bachelor came knocking at Roberta's door and pretty much swept her off her feet—for a few days. She confessed that her new suitor was treating her with the frankness and honesty she believed she wanted. However, his openness in talking about his deep feelings for her and their future together was scaring Roberta to death!

Within a short period, the relationship became much too stressful for her, and she terminated it. Being with such an open and honest person wasn't all that she had imagined it would be. And although she felt guilty about hurting such a wonderful guy, the relief Roberta felt after ending the relationship only reinforced her belief that this wonderful guy wasn't "right" for her.

Could this relationship have worked out? It very well might have if the anxious bachelor had simply exercised a bit more discretion and restraint in his courting endeavors. It is our conviction that the sincere, but naïve, suitor would have won Roberta's heart if he had shown a little more patience and held back any talk of "them" and "their future." Such conversation contained too many implied expectations of commitment, which created stress for Roberta. Her hopeful suitor would have been better off playing it cool in the beginning. As long as stress is present in a relationship, communication will be inhibited, making it difficult for a relationship to grow. What reasonable way is there to keep a relationship as non-threatening and soothing as possible? Avoid any talk that implies commitment to one another, especially during the early stages of the relationship when you're just getting to know one another.

Let's be candid here. It's obvious that you have serious intentions in winning the one you want, or you wouldn't be reading this book in the first place. Just don't go talking about them! It's okay to show that you care through your actions, but show a little restraint when it comes to verbally expressing them. Don't wear your heart on your sleeve. Don't let your conversation indicate that your present or future happiness depends on the person's reciprocation of your feelings. If you let the person know that your future plans include him or her, you run the risk of scaring that person off.

SHOW, DON'T TELL

Don't verbalize your feelings. Hold back, especially in the first few months of active dating. Some things in life are better left unsaid, and this is especially true in romance. It's okay to show that you care. It's okay for the one you want to suspect that you *might* care, but no confirmations, please! Don't *say* it during the early stage of a relationship! This applies to written communication as well as the spoken word. Sending little cards, notes, and letters that express your love will only sabotage your efforts.

People feel trapped and cornered by premature romantic confessions. However obvious your devotion might otherwise seem, it will remain relatively non-threatening until you start talking about it. Once you make a verbal confession of your love, it puts the person to whom you have expressed these feelings on the spot. To continue the relationship after hearing your confession of love signifies a commitment. This puts the person in a position to be charged with "leading you on," if he or she decides to get involved with someone else.

Upon hearing your words of love, the person is faced with a choice of either accepting your love and surrendering his or her freedom, or simply shutting you out. Most people are likely to do what Roberta did, and walk away from a potentially fine relationship. They are not likely to make any permanent commitments until they are good and "hooked." So the message is simple: Don't go sabotaging yourself with premature confessions of devotion.

Remember, people do not run from love. They run from getting cornered into something they're not sure they want yet. Unless sufficient time has elapsed to allow the other person's feelings to grow and become strong, any threat to their freedom is likely to produce psychological barriers.

BECOMING ADDICTED TO LOVE

Many psychologists and counselors have described being in love as a type of addiction. In fact, there is evidence that some of the physical symptoms accompanying romantic love, such as increased heartbeat, sweaty palms, and the feeling of euphoric infatuation, result from the brain's release of phenylethylamines, more commonly known as the "feel-good" hormones.

With the understanding of how love can be considered an addiction, consider the following analogy: When an illegal drug dealer tries to get someone hooked, does he walk up to the potential "client" and say, "Hi, wanna get hooked?" Of course not! He is much more subtle than that! Nobody who is addicted to drugs starts out with the intention of getting hooked. And this holds just as true when it comes to romantic love. Do people jump at opportunities to surrender their freedom? No, but they *do* feel drawn to situations that produce pleasurable feelings. Most are willing to give up some of their freedom only after they are convinced the trade-off is worth it.

So a drug pusher must be subtle and talk about the immediate benefits of drugs, not the long-term cost. He does not say, "How would you like to spend the rest of your life hopelessly dependent on what I have to offer you?" Who would ever accept such a crazy deal? Instead he says, "Hey, wanna feel good? No cost, man. This one's on me." And so, gradually—step by step—a dependency develops.

When it comes to love, if you reveal how much you care about the one you want too soon, it will be looked at as something that requires reciprocation or "payment." This can be very frightening and overwhelming to even the most receptive individuals. Instead, it is better to give the person you're pursuing consistent, caring attention without any verbal indications that you want something back. Eventually, once your special someone is good and hooked, there will be plenty of time to start receiving love in return.

6

Being Irresistibly Likable

Principle: *The more positive and beneficial the experience someone has when interacting with you, the greater that person's desire will be to continue the association.*

---

*C*an you get someone to *like* you? Even though the human mind will not be forced into anything, it most certainly can be led! And if you know the right rules and can apply them appropriately, you can coax practically anyone you choose into enjoying you and looking forward to the pleasure of your company. Countless books have been written on this very subject. Persons of great experience and wisdom agree: The things you do, the way you treat and act towards others, *do* have a bearing on how they think of and act towards you.

14 ❤ *Light Up!*

A grandfather was talking proudly about his grandchildren. Although he made it clear he loved them all, he reluctantly admitted that he was partial to one in particular. "I try not to play favorites," he explained, "but you know how it is. We tend to respond to others the way they act towards us, and the little guy always acts so excited to see me when I come around that I can't help myself!"

This tendency exists in all of us. Haven't you noticed that when someone is particularly happy and excited to see you or talk to you, that you find yourself emotionally uplifted? It is for this very reason that dogs are such popular pets. People love coming home to someone who is excited to see them, even if it's just a tail-wagging, lovable animal that can't talk.

So learn a lesson from "the little guy" and "man's best friend." When the one you want comes around or calls, show some excitement. Light up!

15 *Show Those Pearly Whites (Smile)!*

Tom and Larry, two high school boys, were discussing girls—their favorite subject—when they came to a sudden realization. They both agreed that they were attracted to girls with cute faces, and were trying to decide what determined "cuteness." Suddenly it dawned on them. Cuteness was invariably related to the amount of smiling a girl did.

Think about it. Aren't the people you're most attracted to those who exhibit bright, happy smiles? Even the ones who you may not be particularly interested in become much more attractive when they smile. Why is a smile so powerful? Because it communicates love and acceptance. And making people feel accepted is one of the most powerful ways to influence them. Remember that the instinctive need for acceptance, which we discussed in Chapter 1, is one of the few emotional requirements common to all humans.

Try an experiment. Walk past a number of people and glance at them *without* smiling. Keep a mental tally of how many respond to you. Then walk past a similar number of people, only this time, smile and nod at them as you pass by. You will get a much more positive and gratifying response with the second group (you may even meet somebody special!). By smiling and nodding, you are conveying a reassuring message to others that they are special.

Many people go through life without ever realizing that smiling is one of the most effective keys to being attractive to members of the opposite sex. And it's so simple! A friendly smile can melt even the strongest opposition, like morning frost before the sunshine. It has been said that people can say or do just about *anything* and get away with it, as long as they smile when they do it!

When you have a warm, genuine smile on your face and make good eye contact with others, you'll help them feel at ease. Later, even if they can't remember *what* you talked about, they *will* remember the feeling they had during the conversation. A smile says many things—you're happy, confident, secure. It says you enjoy talking to and being with the person you're with. It also shows that you care enough about that person to make him or her feel comfortable. The best part is that it's *easy* to smile.

A would-be lover without a smile is like a warrior going into battle without a weapon. Armed with a smile, no challenge is too formidable. So always remember that a smile is a powerful, positive tool, and you can never overuse it. To help win the one you want, always include smiles in your romantic arsenal.

16 *Speak with Enthusiasm!*

Enthusiasm is contagious! It breeds excitement in others. It is one of the keys to influencing others in a positive way. Few human beings are immune to its infectious powers. People tend to feel happy and alive when they are around those who are enthusiastic. Such positive feelings contribute to the bonds of friendship that strengthen people's attachments to each other. So when speaking to the one you want, don't just sit there in a lifeless heap. Put some enthusiasm in your voice! Remember, people get bored easily. Any effort you make to liven up your conversations will be appreciated by others, whether they readily show it or not. Enthusiasm is a subtle way of showing that you care, and will endear you to others.

Try not to be too somber or serious. It's so much better to maintain a light, positive attitude. Have a good sense of humor and don't be afraid to laugh freely. You'll also find that others will respond more readily to you if you exhibit a sense of humor. So try to radiate happiness as much as possible. If you're trying to interest somebody in spending time with you, an upbeat, happy attitude is essential. Be animated! Enthusiasm will help make you an enjoyable companion and more desirable to the one you want.

17 *Talk Positively*

The difference between an optimist and a pessimist is that the optimist sees a glass as half full, while the pessimist sees it as half empty. Since, subconsciously, most of us prefer a half glass of *something* over a half glass of *nothing*, it is usually more rewarding to be in the company of the optimist.

No matter where you go in life or what situations you encounter, you'll face opportunities to judge for yourself how full the glass is. Life is filled with plights and predicaments. How you share your view of your circumstances with others will not go unnoticed. If you have a positive outlook, those with whom you come in contact will subconsciously value your friendship dearly. They will enjoy being in your company. Need we point out that this is especially important in making a good impression on the one you want?

When polled about desirable character traits they would like in a future mate, single college students have consistently rated "sense of humor" high on their lists. Interestingly, this does *not* refer to a person's ability to tell jokes effectively. Rather, it conveys their ability to look on the bright side of things—their willingness to laugh at a predicament or serious situation. People who do this are uplifting to be around and, whether they realize it or not, quietly endear themselves to others. It is emotionally rewarding to be in their presence.

18 *Discuss the Other Person's Interests*

Although communication with others is a basic human need, most people do not have great confidence in their abilities to carry on a conversation. If you want your friendship to be highly valued, you must learn how to help others feel comfortable talking with you. Surprisingly, the key to this is not necessarily having an extensive knowledge of many subjects. Rather, it is a willingness to *let others do most of the talking* on any subject that interests *them!* You can draw out anybody in this fashion by assuming the role of a sincere student who is willing to learn from a more informed instructor. Normally, conversation is a subtle kind of tug-of-war. In the usual exchange between two people, each person merely waits for the other to stop talking, before shifting the topic back to one of his or her own preference. If you do this, you are missing a great opportunity to rack up points with the one you want. People experience a sense of self-worth and importance when someone shows an interest in what they have to say. Encouraging others to discuss their interests will make them feel good about themselves. Don't pass up such opportunities!

How can you best achieve this during conversations with the one you want? By asking questions and then listening thoughtfully to the responses. Ask the person about his or her goals, accomplishments, experiences, or attitudes. In short, ask about anything and everything that relates to that individual. It is the one subject on which all people are experts!

American educator and author of *How to Win Friends and Influence People,* Dale Carnegie once reported the case of a bigamist who had captured the hearts (and the bank accounts!) of twenty-three women. When the bigamist was asked how he had gotten so many women to fall in love with him, he responded by saying that it was no problem as long as he got them to talk about themselves. Although, obviously, there was more to it than that, there is also no question that encouraging the women to talk about themselves is a tactic that helped this bigamist win them over. And don't think that women are the only ones who like to do this. Men can be just as vulnerable, if not more!

So when conversing with others, remember to keep their interests your focal point. Strategically, it will help you secure their friendship and set the stage for them to fall deeply in love with you.

19 Use Flattery

Flattery will get you everywhere! It is an *extremely* effective tool for helping you endear yourself to others. But quite often, people hesitate to use flattery for fear that it will be dismissed as insincere. While it's true that many people act suspiciously toward those who pay them flagrant, outright compliments, deep down they are gratefully eating it up. In the words of Paul H. Gilbert, flattery is "the art of telling another person exactly what he thinks of himself."

So don't be fooled by another's skeptical reaction to your compliments. When people seem to resist your flattery, realize that it's just a show on their part. Actually, they are deeply affected by it— more than they'd like you to know. Remember, the human need for appreciation is stronger than the ability to resist it. Therefore, your compliments and words of praise will go a long way in building relationships. Be liberal in offering it.

A word of caution, though. Flattery is very potent, like fine perfume. A little bit goes a long way. Sprinkle it around sparingly and trust it to do its job. Resist the temptation to pour it on. Too much flattery can dilute its effectiveness and undermine your genuine sincerity. People tend to put up psychological barriers and become more resistant when they think they're being "set up" or "put on." But having said that, let us repeat: Your well-placed compliments and words of praise will go a long way in helping to build and strengthen relationships. Use flattery, but use it wisely. It will make you an enjoyable, sought-after companion.

20 *Understay Your Welcome*

It is a commonly understood that, in most cases, hanging around someone for too long can cause you to wear out your welcome. However, if you *understay* your welcome, you can actually leave that person wanting more of you, even if he or she wasn't that interested to begin with! This simple tactic not only eliminates anyone's hesitation to being with you, it also helps create a more positive atmosphere for future get-togethers. People will enjoy your company *more* when you are available *less!*

So be extremely aware of the amount of time you spend with the one you want. Depart while things are still going good, even though you're having a wonderful time and want to stay longer. Be the one who ends the conversations, the phone calls, the dates, or other encounters just a little bit shorter than expected. Just say, "It's time to go . . ." or "I've got to get up early in the morning . . ." or simply, "Goodnight!" No matter how good a time you're having, don't procrastinate ending it. If you wait so long that the other person is the one who initiates the good-bye or good night, you will have wasted an opportunity to become more desirable—a virtual "step back" in winning that person.

21 Be Graceful in the Face of Rejection (as Preparation for Strategic Comeback)

The Music Man is one of the greatest musicals of all time. In it, a traveling flimflam salesman named Harold Hill arrives at River City, Iowa, with the intention of swindling its gullible townspeople. Hill masquerades as a music professor who promises to organize a River City boys' band. After collecting money for instruments that he has no intention of ever delivering, Hill plans to skip town with the money. In order to pull off the scam, though, he must first win the confidence of the townspeople. He starts by romancing Marian, the local librarian and part-time music teacher.

Marian, however, is very suspicious of "Professor" Hill and not easily romanced. Time after time, he approaches her, cheerfully doffing his hat while flashing a smile, but she always gives him the cold shoulder and walks on by. Now, most people would tend to respond negatively if snubbed like that. But not the positive-thinking Harold Hill, who remains undaunted. Through his vast experience in sales, he is confident that a positive attitude and warm smile will eventually break down the walls of resistance that separate him from Marian. He consistently responds to her temporary rejection with a confident but humble response and a big smile. And, sure enough, in the end she succumbs to his charm.

Professor Hill shows us how to win the one we want by being graceful in the face of apparent rejection. Real life is like that, too.

Those who are willing to lose some small battles graciously, will end up impressively winning big wars!

DEALING WITH THE SKIDS

One of the most important things taught in a driver's education class is how to regain control of your vehicle when it starts to skid out of control. "Turn *into* the slide!" students are instructed again and again. So it is with relationships.

Let's say you have a clear idea of where you want the relationship to go, but you can feel the person slip-sliding away. This is not the time to stubbornly turn towards your goal with even more determination, for this would more likely throw the entire relationship into a spinout! It's better to temporarily "go with the flow," than it is to resist the slide. If the person you want doesn't seem ready to accept the same degree of involvement that you do, then it's better for you to appear willing to accept whatever degree he or she wants. In reality, this doesn't mean that you're willing to give up your original plans for the relationship any more than the driver of a vehicle is willing to slide into a ditch. But sometimes, you have to turn in that direction just long enough to regain control. Then you can gently guide the one you want back to you.

When you are turned down in your request for a date or brushed off in a conversation, don't turn off your charm. Turn it on stronger! Smile even bigger! Be willing to bow out temporarily with a smile and parting words of kindness and good will. It is this kind of behavior on your part that will convince others that the friendship you offer is genuine, sincere, and worth having. People can't help but love and admire someone who is gracious in the face of apparent defeat. Losing gracefully will subconsciously induce others to be trusting of you in the future. And, remember, love is based on trust.

7

Exhibiting Self-Mastery and Leadership Ability

Principle: *People respect and are subconsciously drawn to those who exhibit qualities of aloofness and independence. They are turned off by those who manifest tendencies to cling.*

Obviously, it's important in romance to exhibit very positive and accepting attitudes towards those whom you desire. But you must never appear as though you would allow your feelings for the other person to compromise your self-respect. You must not surrender your decision-making abilities or independence in an effort to please the one you want. Remember this: It's practically impossible for a person to experience romantic feelings for anyone they can manipulate like a puppet! Most people find that as soon as they have someone wrapped around their little finger, they lose interest. The thrill of being chased is gone. The challenge is over. The romance is destroyed.

So if you want to be loved romantically, it is of paramount importance to demonstrate that you are an independent, self-respecting person who will not be taken for granted. Convey that you make your own decisions and are not easily swayed from your principles, even for love. Furthermore, it is critical to demonstrate that you will not tolerate disrespect. If people feel that they can walk all over you and get away with it, this, too, will dampen their desire for you. The love tactics found in this chapter will help guide you in establishing your independence and commanding the respect that is so essential for romantic love.

22 *Plan Out Dates*

One of the easiest ways to exhibit your leadership and independence to the one you want is to have a plan when it comes to your dates. Never give the mistaken impression that you are content to let things just happen. Show some initiative. Plan out the details of your date— know where you're going, what you'll be doing, and how long it will take. Don't leave these things to chance, or it will appear as if you're not in control and clueless about your own objectives. People are drawn to those who exhibit a sense of where they are going. Having definite goals in mind for each date will demonstrate your ability to act as an independent agent. It will help you earn the respect of others.

Of course, this doesn't mean you should be selfish! It's always a good idea to consult the other person when making plans. Get some input, and if he or she wants to do something other than what you have in mind, don't be stubborn. You can still demonstrate an active role by offering options, or considering their ideas and coming to a mutual agreement. And if, by chance, you're not the person initiating the date, don't remain passive. Contribute a suggestion or two that might add to the enjoyment of the date. Remember, showing leadership doesn't necessarily mean you must initiate *everything*, but it does mean that, at the very least, you should show some interest in knowing the plan.

23 *Demonstrate Independent Thinking*

One of the things people actually seek from a romantic relationship, whether they realize it or not, is someone to lean on and draw strength from during life's frightening and distressing moments. Because of this, people are instinctively attracted to those who appear emotionally strong.

Think of a situation in which you would need someone to talk to—when you're upset, or have an important decision to make, or are feeling lonely. Who would you rather talk to? Someone who is independent, levelheaded, and a clear thinker? Or someone who is characteristically indecisive and dependent? If you are like most, you'll be attracted to the person you sense is strong. People want *to lean,* not *be leaned on!* So it follows that if you want to attract others to you in a long-term relationship, it's important to demonstrate the ability to do your own thinking and make decisions in your associations with others. Show that you are strong enough to lean on. There are several ways you can do this, including being decisive, speaking your mind, and occasionally being contrary.

BE DECISIVE

When given choices, be decisive. If your date asks where you'd like to go for dinner or what movie you'd like to see, don't respond with, "I don't know; you decide," or "I don't care; whatever you want." Try to offer a suggestion (even if such matters appear trivial and you really don't care). These are opportunities that demonstrate your willingness to share in the decision-making, and should not be wasted. When dating, many people näively defer all of the choices in small matters back to their dates. They don't realize that, little by little, they are compromising their image as an equal—as someone who can be depended on for emotional support and strength. You'll command greater respect and become more attractive by simply making your own choices.

SPEAK YOUR MIND

Speak your mind! Offer your opinions in a discussion, even if you feel they may be outlandish or controversial. Don't come across as someone with no opinions of your own. If the one you want senses that you are easily intimidated or afraid to say what's on your mind, it's a good bet that he or she will lose respect for you. Feel confident in joining in a conversation without worrying that others may think you are wrong or find you boring because of it. You will actually make "points" by exhibiting such an independent attitude.

Never feel that your opinions have to agree with those of others. *Be your own person!* Be comfortable saying what you think, even if it is contrary to the opinions of the person or persons you are with. Don't be afraid to stand alone! Nothing is more attractive than someone who has the courage to stand up for his or her convictions. This does *not* mean that you should be arrogant or unpleasant in doing so. It is certainly possible to pleasantly disagree. And never try to force someone else to accept your ideas.

BE CONTRARY ONCE IN A WHILE

Be contrary sometimes. Don't always go along with everything your date wants and suggests. You won't be adequately respected if you do. Don't allow anyone to get the impression that you could be easily led around, as if you had a ring through your nose! This isn't to say you shouldn't compromise in the relationship, just don't be complacent and go along with every decision the other person makes. If your date wants to see the latest action movie, but you're in the mood for a comedy, make it known. And even if you end up going to see that action flick anyway, at least your date will respect the fact that you weren't afraid to be a little contrary by offering a different suggestion. By maintaining your own course instead of blindly following another person's every whim, your desirability will be enhanced.

To sum it up, be honest, open, and forthright. Don't be afraid to manifest independent thinking. It is one of the keys to fulfilling romance!

24 *Communicate Your Personal Destiny*

A young man who was having a hard time winning the girl of his dreams sat down after a particularly uninspiring date. "What am I doing wrong?" he wondered. He couldn't quite put his finger on it, but finally concluded that he couldn't go on any longer centering his life around *her.* He decided that no matter what happened, he was going to maintain the attitude that he still had a special goal in life to accomplish, whether she loved him back or not. If she wanted to accompany him on that mission, she could be part of it. If not, that was fine, too, because he would go on to fulfill it *without her!*

Although his determination was mostly a final attempt to salvage as much of his self-esteem as possible, it resulted in an amazing turn of events. He began to act in a way that said, "I'm going somewhere in life, with or without you." This new attitude inadvertently demonstrated his emotional independence to his girl, heightening her interest in him almost immediately. Eventually, he won her love! It's much easier to fall in love with a person who is going somewhere in life regardless of what you do, than it is with someone who is basing his or her entire future on you.

Fifteenth-century French leader Joan of Arc once declared to one of her generals, "I will lead the men over the wall." His response was, "Not a man will follow you." But Joan, independent and determined, didn't care. She replied, "I will not look back to see whether anyone is following or not!" She won the unwavering love and devotion of her soldiers by exhibiting this very attitude.

In your quest for love and devotion, be like Joan of Arc! Fearlessly share the vision of your life's mission with the one you want, making sure to convey your intention and willingness to do it alone if necessary. Such an attitude will inspire the person you desire to want you in return.

25 *Be Unpredictable*

A prominent psychologist, when speaking to an assembly of college students some years ago, remarked that one of the things people need most in their lives to be happy is a little variety. To coin a phrase, "Variety is the spice of life." It provides mental stimulation and keeps us interested in continuing with life's sometimes wearisome struggle. Without it, life can be dull, uninteresting, and boring.

Sometimes we fail to realize just how prone human beings are to becoming bored, and therefore, how willingly they will allow themselves to be drawn to someone who shows promise of keeping life interesting. So do the unexpected from time to time! Maintaining some mystery and keeping people unsure of your next move will keep their interest in you heightened. This doesn't mean that you shouldn't behave dependably most of the time. It just means that, every once in a while, you should try to surprise people by doing something a little different from what they are anticipating.

Some examples? Surprise your special someone with a gift for no reason and at a time when he or she would least expect it. When they think they have you hooked, *ignore them;* and when they begin to feel that you don't care anymore, *suddenly drop by for a visit!* How often have you heard someone who is passionately crazy about another say, "I just can't figure him (or her) out!"? Occasional surprises help keep people hooked. So do the unexpected! Be unpredictable! Be nice to them when they're cruel to you, and when they treat you nice, don't be afraid to act a little indifferently. Keep 'em guessing. It'll keep them interested.

26 *Act Indifferently to What They Think of You*

A couple we'll call Phil and Justine had been seeing each other for a while, and a romance was beginning to bud. Phil was particularly intrigued by Justine's independent attitudes. One night, however, she lost her appeal. They had been discussing some controversial issue, and Justine boldly stated her opinion. Phil happened to disagree with her and said so, yet the strength of Justine's convictions made her even more attractive to him than before.

His sudden fascination, however, was short-lived. When Justine realized that Phil disagreed with her, she quickly backed down and actually apologized for expressing herself in such a forthright manner. Most damaging of all, though, she admitted her concern to Phil that he might think less of her for having such an opinion.

Can you see the irony? Only a moment before, Phil had actually respected Justine's ability to stand up for what she believed in. But then she became apologetic, and fell off the pedestal Phil had just put her on. In other words, she blew it! If only she had continued acting indifferently to what Phil might have thought of her, he would have continued adoring her! And although Phil disagreed with her opinion, he would have still felt respect for her. (And remember, *respect* is one of the essential elements necessary for falling in love.) But as soon as Justine exhibited a willingness to back down and compromise her independence *simply to please him,* she lost esteem in his eyes. It became obvious to Phil that she was willing to compromise the integrity of who she was just to please him. His growing infatuation was squelched, and a potentially fine relationship went down the drain.

So, in your associations with others, don't let on that you care in the least what they think of you. While deep down it may disturb you to think you're being judged, you will command respect by acting indifferently to it all. The minute people realize that you care about what they think of you, they'll judge you more harshly. They'll lose respect. Human nature causes us to be turned off by those who compromise themselves to please us, and drawn to those who appear indifferent.

A popular song from a few years back asked, "Why did you have to be a heartbreaker, when I was being what you want me to be?" The answer is, because you can't have romantic feelings for someone you don't respect, *and you can't respect those who are willing to remake themselves to please you!* In the beginning, romance thrives on the appearance of an indifferent, carefree attitude two people have towards each other. This is one of those fundamental principles of human behavior.

27 Don't Fish for Feedback

When caught up in the agonies of a romantic pursuit, particularly during the early stages, it's only natural to want to find out where you stand with the other person. What does that person think of you? Is he or she experiencing the same anxieties that you are? At times, the urge to seek some sign of reciprocation will become almost too strong to resist, but you must not to yield to this temptation. Fishing for feedback is definitely detrimental to your romantic health!

There are two fundamental problems with sending up trial balloons to get a reading on someone's romantic feelings for you. First, any feedback you may get in the beginning stages of a relationship is an unreliable indication of a person's true feelings anyway. Most people, especially early in a relationship, aren't clear about what they are really feeling yet. It is very possible that a person is growing to love you but is not yet consciously aware of it. The transition from a subconscious to a conscious awareness of love normally takes time. It will inevitably occur if you don't become discouraged and give up prematurely.

Second, probing to find out a person's feelings for you is a clear signal that you're hoping for reciprocation. This makes you appear needy, excessively vulnerable, and emotionally fragile. It signals that you're vulnerable to rejection and not dealing from a position of emotional strength. This, in turn, has the unfortunate effect of undermining their feelings of respect and diminishing their romantic interest in you.

Until you're absolutely sure you've won that person over, don't ask about or act concerned with his or her romantic feelings toward you. Seeking assurances of affection only communicates emotional insecurity on your part, and destroys the kind of respect another person needs to burn with desire for you. Ironically, the more aloof you appear about the other person's attitude towards you, the better your chances of earning his or her respect and love.

28 *Show Anger When Appropriate*

If you've ever been dumped by someone and can't remember ever chastising that person somewhere along the way, then you may have lost the relationship unnecessarily. Does this sound strange? Well, it's true. Although it's usually best to be agreeable and pleasant when trying to build a relationship, there are times when being complacent is not the best course to pursue. To elevate the relationship beyond the level of being "just friends," you need to demonstrate your ability to get angry with the person when the situation calls for it. A good, verbal chewing out is sometimes the only way to show the one you want that you are, after all, independent-minded and worth respecting. Showing anger is sometimes necessary for a happy relationship.

Can you imagine a child growing up without the need for occasional chastisement? Of course not! Having someone on hand to enforce behavioral limits is a necessary part of a happy and secure childhood. Well, the same applies to adults, who are just kids themselves in grown-up bodies. And adults, too, need to be reproved and put in their proper place from time to time. Your partner will be much happier and, yes, more secure, knowing that you're not afraid to stand up and show anger when he or she is out of line.

Listen to Lee's explanation concerning the difference between Karen, the girl he couldn't live without, and all the previous girls in his life, who were incapable of stirring him to that same level of devotion, "Karen is the first girl in my life," he said, "who has ever stood up to me!" This ability to stand up to the one you want and express anger if that person abuses your feelings or otherwise takes you for granted is an essential key to romantic love. Nobody can really get excited about you if they're not secretly just a little afraid of crossing you! This is one of the best-kept secrets of romantic love. Make note of it. Do, however, follow these guidelines when expressing anger:

■ **Don't scold prematurely.** To prevent being taken for granted, you have only one real tool at your disposal—the unspoken threat of losing you. But this is not a threat unless there has been enough time for bonding. This is why you must not chastise or reprove the one you want until a strong bond of friendship exists between you first. And such a bond occurs only by spending plenty of time together. If you attempt to show anger or displeasure before such a bond exists, this tactic will backfire. Use the same strategy as that of a man who successfully makes the transition to becoming a stepfather. If he tries to discipline the children before he has spent adequate time showing them love and positive attention, the discipline will simply be resented. But if he has first laid a foundation of love and has exercised proper patience before laying down the law, his disciplinary measures will ultimately be effective.

■ **Don't fight over petty, irrelevant issues.** The only time to show anger is over basic disrespect or disregard for your feelings. (This is the only justified claim you can bring against another person anyway. You have no right to sit in judgment on other matters.) Express your disappointment by saying something like, "Hey, I've taken just about all the lack of consideration I'm going to take! You've been taking me for granted (or mistreating me), and I refuse to put up with that kind of treatment from anybody—*even you!"*

■ **Don't stick around to give the person the opportunity to fight with you.** Don't argue. State your case, show anger while doing it, *and then depart!* Leave them alone to give your words a chance to sink in. The truth will justify you. Getting sucked into a verbal ping-pong match will only weaken the otherwise very powerful effect this tactic can have. You'll be surprised at its power. Remember, *reason* doesn't motivate human beings—*emotion* does. Once you get the emotional pendulum moving, it will eventually swing your way. Employing this tactic will strengthen your influence; however, it *must* be used in conjunction with Love Tactic #29. Read on . . .

29 *Show Forgiveness After Expressing Anger*

Yes, you *can* gain a person's respect by standing up to and chastising them when they deserve it! But it's *absolutely essential* for you to demonstrate kind and charitable feelings towards that person afterwards—that is, if you don't want to destroy the foundation of friendship you have already established. Human beings are extremely sensitive to chastisement, and the one you want is no exception. Take steps to reassure the person you've stood up to that you hold no grudges and you're still friends. If you don't, it won't be long before that person will despise you.

Therefore, as soon as your angry words have had a chance to sink in, take steps to show the rebuked person that, although your reaction was strong, you're still loyal. You still care. Don't apologize or act as though your anger wasn't justified. (It most certainly *was!*) This is not the time to back down and start acting like your anger was a mistake. Just seek out the person's company, put the incident behind you, and resume the relationship.

The other person will, in most cases, act a bit standoffish at first, even if he or she knows that your anger was justified. It's a matter of hurt pride. After all, the truth can hurt. But don't be discouraged! Show persistence, if necessary, to renew the relationship. Amiable feelings will soon return. It'll become evident that your friendship is unconditional and that you intend to be their *true friend*. When this happens, your relationship with the one you want will take a big step toward romantic fulfillment. This is the same principle that causes two kids to become best friends after clearing the air with an after-school fist fight!

8

Cultivating Their Emotional Dependence

Principle: *People become emotionally "hooked"
on those rare persons who can satisfy their
ongoing need for human understanding.*

---

*T*here is a big difference between *loving* and being *in love*. If you *love* someone, you're still in control of your emotions—you choose how you'll allow yourself to feel about and react towards that individual. If you have fallen *in love*, however, you are no longer calling the shots. You become hopelessly dependent upon (and at the mercy of) whomever you've allowed yourself to fall for. The key here to winning the one you want is to get that person to become emotionally dependent on you—*not* the other way around!

Have you ever wondered why it is so common for patients to fall in love with their psychotherapists? It's because there is a very real tendency for people to fall in love with those who satisfy their emotional needs. In effective counseling sessions, clients find their needs for compassionate understanding are being met, perhaps for the first time. They find themselves becoming willingly dependent on their counselors for a continued satisfaction of those needs. They become psychologically "hooked."

Likewise, as you learn to satisfy a person's deep emotional need for understanding, you will find that, with time, that person will become emotionally dependent on you! Being successful at love sometimes requires playing the part (to some degree) of a good therapeutic counselor. The better you fulfill this role, the deeper the love will be from the one you want. The following tactics will help you successfully accomplish this.

30 *Actually Be There (In Person!)*

When Sir Edmund Hillary was asked what compelled him to climb mountains, he responded, "Because they're there!" This same principle is applicable to love. The fact is that people tend to fall in love with those who are personally available—"because they're there!" Being there in the flesh plays a large role in getting someone to fall in love with you.

The first requirement is to make yourself available to the one you want. Although this may not always be easy, try to make your presence known and *felt*. You must not be afraid of "intruding" to some degree into that person's life. Sometimes the greatest love is found, not because we went out and actively sought it, but because somebody pushed it on us at a time when we thought we weren't yet interested. When people buy, it is always from the salesman who was there to sell to them. And when people are ready to fall in love, it will always be with someone who is relatively close at hand!

One enterprising young college student made use of this principle while courting his future wife. When he called her dorm and she wasn't there, he would always leave a message with her roommate. This kept her constantly aware of his proximity. (But he never let her think she had him all sewed up, either. Often when she'd return his call, he'd be out with someone else.)

So be there for the one you want—even if they don't seem to need or want you at the moment! The time will come when they *will* need someone—and you'll be there to step in! Like the patient who has come to depend on his therapist in a time of crisis, the one you want will also turn to *you* in his or her hour of need.

Keep in mind the underlying message of all advertising: "If you're in a buying mood, I've got something to sell!" Whether it is an unexpected visit, a quick phone call, or just a note letting the person know you're thinking about them, such small acts of kindness will eventually result in their emotional dependence on you.

The necessity of actually being there in person in order to win the one you want cannot be overemphasized. *Personal, face-to-face contact is vital.* Some people try to develop relationships subtly (by sending notes and cards, for example) but this rarely works. It's the chicken's way out! Building a relationship requires the courage to personally face the one you want, and this is something that cannot be accomplished from a distance.

Sure, there are stories of people who met and corresponded by mail at one point in their courtship and are happily married today. But this is only part of the picture. In order for someone to really fall in love with you, they've got to get to know you first. Remember, "to know you is to love you," and getting to know you requires personal, face-to-face contact. Why do you think there is such a high incidence of romance in the workplace? It's because work throws people into situations in which they are constantly together, and this lays the groundwork for relationships to develop. You don't have to work with someone before he or she will fall in love with you, but you *do* have to spend time with that person!

31 *Listen Reflectively*

People want someone they can confide in. They really do! They are happiest and function best when there's at least one other person who really knows and understands what they're going through. Notwithstanding this fact, many people seem to have a hard time revealing their true thoughts and feelings to others. How often have you heard a frustrated but caring partner in a rocky relationship lament, "I beg him [her] to tell me what's wrong, but he [she] just clams up and keeps it inside!" Many people find it difficult to open up, even to this kind of sincere prodding.

What can you do to win someone's trust and break down the

communication barriers? Use a method known as *reflective listening.* How? By following these guidelines:

1. **Remain silent while the other person is speaking.** Don't interrupt. Let the person talk as long as he or she wants. The more willing you are to allow the other person to speak freely, the more completely you'll help satisfy their emotional need to be understood. This also encourages the person's honesty and openness.

2. **Keep your body still.** Fidgeting conveys impatience and disinterest. You know how important body language is, right? Well, fidgeting can prevent the speaker from speaking openly.

3. **Acknowledge what is being said.** When the speaker pauses for some sign that you're really listening and understanding, just nod your head. Restrict your comments to such things as "Mm-hmm" or "Yes, go on . . ." As one man explained it, "I don't want sympathy or advice. I just want a listening ear."

4. **Keep your eyes focused on the person who is talking.** Not looking at the person or failing to maintain eye contact implies that you're not interested in what is being said. You can't expect people to open up to you if it appears that you're not truly interested.

5. **Occasionally, when the speaker pauses for some response from you, briefly sum up (in your own words, if possible) what you feel the person is trying to say.** Try to describe their feelings even *more accurately* than they themselves have. The objective here is to rephrase what the person has told you in such a way that he or she, amazed at your perceptivity, says, "Exactly!" or "Right!" or some other affirmation that you really understand what they are saying. This process will help the speaker to more clearly identify his or her own feelings, while experiencing a sense of unity with you.

      How about an example?

TIM: You know, I've had it with the people at my office!

TINA: Go on . . .

TIM: All they ever do anymore is pick, pick, pick on everything I try to do!

TINA: Sounds as if you're upset because the people at work are overly critical.

TIM: You got it! They're anxious to jump down my throat for practically nothing, but they never notice anything good that I do.

TINA: Kind of like they're quick to criticize you for trivial, unimportant things, while totally overlooking your positive accomplishments?

TIM: That's exactly the way it is!

Once you can get the one you want to respond positively to your summation of his or her feelings, you can be sure that you're on the right track to winning their heart. You'll be surprised at how anxious people will be to continue opening up to you when you make them feel understood. Believe it or not, this simple technique can keep people talking about themselves and their feelings for hours. They will have a difficult time breaking themselves away from the conversation because they have never before felt such affirmation in their lives! It even works with those people who are normally withdrawn and incapable of such communication.

6. **Don't evaluate or give any opinions regarding the person's attitudes or feelings.** This takes a lot of practice and self-discipline, but don't do it. Don't sit in judgment. Don't criticize! But don't sympathize either! Just try to be objective. Any opinions from you at all (either negative *or* positive) may cause the person to regret having opened up to you. The doors of communication will then close. But why not show sympathy? Because even sympathy is a type of judgment. It says that you've stopped listening with the pure intent to just understand, and have begun evaluating before the person has had a chance to feel fully understood. It casts doubts on your objectivity, even if it is a bias in their favor. After

all, if you're not completely fair *this* time, how can they have confidence that *next* time, *after they've opened up their soul to you*, they won't find themselves on the opposite side of your good graces? That's emotionally frightening, and will prevent a person from revealing on a deeper level, where you could have even greater influence. Furthermore, you will have deprived them of the enriching experience of being purely understood, which is one of the most loving experiences a human being can ever have.

7. **Allow others to open up at their own pace.** Don't push. If they seem to wander illogically in their conversation, let them! Don't try to direct their thoughts back to where *you* believe they should go. Just try to understand the main gist of the conversation from moment to moment. If they want to stop talking altogether, fine! Be willing to accept that. Don't dig for information the person may not yet be ready to reveal. By providing a non-threatening atmosphere in which others can express themselves at will, without fear of criticism or judgment, you'll soon be the one who others will seek out "just to talk." This kind of patient listening is rare indeed, and others will soon recognize that being with you quenches a life-long emotional thirst. Satisfying this need to be understood is perhaps the greatest secret to winning love.

Commit these guidelines to memory. Practice them in your relationships with others. The more understanding you provide for the one you want, the greater influence you'll have with that person. In addition, he or she will become more strongly attached to you. The importance of reflective listening as a tool in your arsenal to win love cannot be emphasized enough. It is perhaps *the most essential tactic of all* to include in your overall strategy for successful romance. Using reflective listening skills will increase your influence with people immeasurably—especially the one you want!

32 *Avoid Being Critical*

Although certain practices are essential for success in love, there are others that must be *avoided*. What's one of the biggest no-no's? *Giving criticism!* Although people invariably try to justify this action by claiming that they're merely trying to help the person "improve," the sad fact is that it very rarely has this effect.

Experience has shown that the only predictable result of criticism is the weakening of trust in human relationships. Occasionally, of course, a person may take a critical remark to heart and make some beneficial changes because of it, but it *still* makes them less willing to open up to the person who did the criticizing. And if you're trying to win someone's love, this loss of trust is completely self-defeating. *Let someone else point out their faults if they wish, but don't you do it!*

Consider your own feelings. Think about the last time someone offered you some so-called "constructive criticism." How did you react? (Be honest, now!) Not too well, right? Even if the critical observations were true, they were undoubtedly painful! What happened afterwards? Did the experience increase your feelings of fondness for that individual? Of course not! Even those who don't show their hurt still *feel* it, and they won't be anxious to repeat such an experience. So it will be only a matter of time before they'll start avoiding their critic. *Don't let that critic be you!*

Sometimes, if you're not careful, you could be critical without even realizing it. Although you can generally guard against doing this by first asking yourself, "How would I feel if someone were to say this to me?" there are still a few subtle ways of criticizing that we need to warn you against. They are:

- **Asking "Why?"** Specifically, avoid use of this three-letter word. If you want to really set someone on edge, try using this single-word interrogative about five times in a row in casual conversation. But do so at your own risk! If you end up in the hospital, we'll have to assume that you've underestimated the maddening effect this little word can have on people. But don't say we didn't warn you! There is something about the word "why" when seeking information that automatically causes a defensive response. By using it, you unintentionally demand others to justify themselves to you, or to justify their perceptions of things.

Think about it. Perhaps this is why it can become so exasperating to an adult when a little child asks an endless stream of "whys." Although the adult may do his best to give a satisfying answer, he is still on the hot seat of having to justify the reasons things are the way they are. It is stressful and rouses emotional defenses. Then, after having done his best to provide a satisfactory explanation, the child is likely to turn around and ask "why" again. The adult may not even realize why this is such an irritation, but the reason is that his whole value system is put on trial each time that question is asked. With that one little word "why," the child has successfully made himself the judge, and the grown-up the defendant. And that can be exasperating!

If you sincerely want to understand someone's reason for doing a certain thing or believing a certain way without any intention of passing judgment on their motives, try to soften your interrogation so it shows that you simply want *to understand*, not *judge*. You can usually do this by cautiously asking, "Could you help me understand how this seems to be the case?" or "Could you help me understand the reasons that such a course of action seems best?" This type of questioning, while still seeking information, does so in a less threatening way, which helps show your willingness to assume good faith on the other person's part, and a desire to understand rather than to judge. You'll find it very effective in preventing the one you want from feeling criticized. This simple practice of avoiding the use of "why" in your conversations will give you an added edge in your challenge to win someone's heart.

■ **Giving advice.** As the proverb goes, "Don't give advice. Wise men don't need it, and fools won't heed it." But we must add, most everyone *will* resent it! All advice says, in effect, "You know what you oughta do? Well, *since you don't have the brains to figure it out for yourself*, let me tell you . . ." The very giving of advice, in itself, implies that those being offered it are deficient in reasoning ability, and that can be extremely demeaning.

Be aware that it is easy to get tricked into giving advice. People may come to you asking, "What should I do?" In such cases, it's easy to think that you can make an exception to the rule of not giving advice, since they asked. *But don't fall for that old trick!* What they *really* need is someone who will reflectively listen to them. If you don't believe this, just think about how many people in your own life have already ignored your advice—even when they came begging for it in the first place. This is because people already know in the back of their minds what they should do. Knowing *what* to do has never been the problem. They're just experiencing some sort of subconscious conflict about actually *doing it! That's* the problem! And by telling them again what they should do, when they don't really want to do it, only enhances their sense of conflict, guilt, and consequently, resentment towards you for tormenting them further So save your breath—and advice. What people really want when they ask for advice is a listening ear.

By listening reflectively and becoming a sounding board, you allow others to work out their problems themselves. This affirms people's sense of self-worth, and when the one you want experiences this coming from you it increases their love for you.

■ **Claiming it's not your intention to be critical.** Masking your criticism by claiming it isn't your intention can be the worst form of criticism. It feigns friendship, but proves disloyalty. It goes like this, "I don't mean this to be critical, *but . . .*" It's hard to avoid a tightening of your stomach muscles when these words are directed to you. The person doing the criticizing may näively think that qualifying the statements in this way somehow makes them less offensive. Wrong! We are often hurt *more* by someone who pretends to be a friend and then criticizes us, than by a proven enemy who has been openly hostile all along.

These subtle forms of criticism are by no means the only ones you may be utilizing without realizing it. They are just a few examples. Be on constant guard to keep from using them. The moral of the story? If you want to be loved, *don't criticize!* The less you indulge in criticism, the easier it will be for others, including the one you want, to love you. Remember it!

33 *Express Genuine Admiration and Praise*

Over the years, marital counselors have learned some great lessons about behavior through their first-hand observations of human relationships. One such lesson, for example, is that the intensity of love one person feels towards another in a relationship is in direct proportion to how important and worthwhile they believe they are in the eyes of that other person. In other words, *the more important a person feels that he or she really is to you, the stronger and deeper will be their reciprocated feelings of love, dependence, and attachment for you.*

THE VALUE OF FEELING VALUABLE

One of the most important human needs, next to feeling unconditional acceptance, is to feel valuable. Everyone needs to feel important. Don't *you?* Don't you need to feel that you have real worth? People not only need to feel accepted in spite of their faults, but also to be recognized and appreciated for their positive qualities.

Only others can satisfy this type of emotional need. Effectual praise and recognition cannot be self-administered! Self-praise is just too shallow. No matter how much a person tells himself "I'm great!" another voice deep inside echoes back, "Who do you think you're kidding? Can't you see that your credibility is flawed—your motive is suspect?"

Objectivity is the first requirement of a credible judgment. And deep down, all of us intuitively realize that it is impossible to be emotionally detached and objective about ourselves. Just as nature has made it so humans are not able to see their own faces (without looking in a mirror, of course), it has also denied them the ability to objectively view their own characters. *We need others!* It is only through others that we can comprehend our own existence. Like blind men, we depend on others to tell to us what we "look" like. If there is anything virtuous, lovely, or praiseworthy in our character, it must first be described to us by someone who is willing to be our "eyes." We cannot trust our own judgment in such matters. As humans, we are dependent on others for effective affirmation of our intrinsic worth.

Now how does all of this tie in with winning that special someone? The person you want is a human being with a need for admiration and praise—just like everybody else—and that need is just crying out for someone like you to satisfy it. By exploiting the opportunity to satisfy this hunger in the one you want, he or she will develop a deeper dependence on you.

THE REASSURANCE OF BEING REASSURED

Most people are starving for emotional reassurance! That's why your effective expressions of genuine admiration for another will go far in cultivating that person's love for you. In spite of popular teachings to the contrary, the truth is that the opinions of others always have more effect on what we think of ourselves than our own self-affirmations. Patting yourself on the back all day long will not result in even one fraction of the confidence that you will feel from a single pat from another person who says, "Well done, John!" or "Good job, Sue!" Thus, recognition of our positive virtues *must* come from another person if it is really going to mean anything. By expressing genuine admiration and praise to the one you want, you'll be meeting an emotional need that he or she is incapable of satisfying alone.

ADMIRING ADMIRINGLY

Now that you're aware of the importance of admiring the one you want, you need to be aware of three points in order to express genuine admiration effectively.

First, it is necessary to establish credibility. You must somehow convince the person that your appraisal has real merit. You must be able to persuade him or her that you are not doling out praise due to a mere sense of loyalty. You must convince that individual that you are always cautious and discerning before making judgments, otherwise your praise won't mean as much. So how is this credibility established? By spending time listening to and getting to know the person *before* you begin expressing things you admire about him or her. Earlier in the book, you read about the use of flattery to enhance your likability. Although flattery *should* be sincere, it may be regarded as a premature evaluation, and perhaps rightly so. Herein lies the inherent problem with flattery—both the giver *and* receiver usually recognize these kinds of compliments as superficial observations made in passing. Flattery alone, therefore, won't satisfy a person's deeper emotional needs. How can you get your words of praise to touch the one you want? By first investing the time to *really understand* the person. If you want your praise to come across as sincere, you must first spend time getting to know the *real* person behind the mask through reflective, non-judgmental listening.

Second, once you've shown your sincerity by investing time and effort to get to know the real person, you must make a mental inventory of that person's good qualities. Everyone has traits that are worthy of admiration. *Every* coin has two sides. When you search hard enough, you'll find that deep down, most people have good intentions and mean well. And even certain negative behaviors are usually distorted forms of a positive trait. A marriage counselor once pointed out to the wife of a closet alcoholic that her husband's sneakiness was just a twisted form of creativity, while his tendency to indulge in self-pity was evidence of an undeveloped ability for compassion. She then admitted that his job *did* require much creativity. And she had always noticed how quick he was to show concern for others. Everyone has good qualities waiting to be discovered. Find them.

Third, once you have found those admirable qualities, tell the person what you have discovered and observed. Offer praise. Express how much you feel you have benefited from their association. The person will see how important he or she is to you. You'll encourage that individual to depend on you for a greater sense of worth. And this, in turn, will draw you one step closer to a fulfilling love relationship!

34 Supply Sympathy

Everyone needs some sympathy from time to time. Those who pretend to be above this need are usually the ones most susceptible to be touched by it. By offering sympathy to the one you want in a time of need, you help relieve his or her emotional burden and strengthen the bonds of attachment that he or she feels for you. People naturally gravitate towards those who help them through emotionally difficult times.

Since sympathy is a form of personal judgment (although a positive one), the rule for giving it is the same as the rule for giving praise: *Do not give it prematurely!* The Bible says, "He that answereth a matter before he heareth it, it is folly and shame unto him." Spend time trying to understand how the person really feels before offering words of intended comfort. Otherwise, the sympathy you give will appear shallow and won't have the lasting impact you want it to. Sympathy should be given only *after* a deeper level of mutual understanding has been reached through empathic, non-judgmental listening. What does that mean? *Listen reflectively first!* Then, after your sincere effort to understand the person without judgment, offer your sympathy. By laying such a foundation beforehand, your sympathy will be much more meaningful and appreciated.

The word *sympathy* means "together in feeling." People need to know they're not alone in how they think and feel. All you need to say is something along the lines of, "You know, I don't blame you a bit for feeling that way. I'd feel the same way under similar circumstances."

Easy, isn't it? Whether it's fear, anger, or just plain emotional pain that is burdening the one you want, reassuring statements of sympathy will work wonders in restoring that person to a happier state of mind. This can't help but make him or her more emotionally dependent on you. Don't neglect opportunities to supply sympathy. It's another key to winning the one you want!

9

Shaking Their Confidence

Principle: *The more insecure someone feels about where they stand with you, the more vulnerable they will be to your romantic advances, and the more intensely they will desire you.*

People can never fully appreciate someone's love if they are allowed to take that love for granted. There must be some ongoing apprehension that the love so freely given could be lost at any time. Always remember this: *While people tend to lack respect for that which they have in the palm of their hand, they become absolutely frantic with desire over that which they may already possess but are in danger of losing!*

Therefore, to successfully stir up someone's romantic passions for you, you must create some uncertainty on their part regarding your feelings for them. It is necessary to instill in their mind a gnawing fear that, in spite of your general appearances of devotion, you're still constantly on the verge of changing your mind about the relationship. Pop singer Billy Joel reminds us that "when you love someone, you're always insecure." Therefore, to make this principle work on your behalf, the one you want must be led to believe that at any given moment you could be lost forever! This properly sets the stage for romantic passion to flourish and true love to blossom.

Insecurity is the mother of infatuation. Doubt is the key to unleashing another person's full potential to ache with romantic passion for you. So, in the midst of the garden of love and friendship that you cultivate, plant a few seeds of doubt. This will keep them wondering if they really *do* have you, after all. The tactics in this chapter suggest ways to do this.

35 *Use Silence*

What do you think would happen if you unexpectedly stopped talking to your partner in the middle of a date and suddenly became very silent during the remainder of your time together? This simple technique can be one of your most subtle and effective ways to tune up a relationship. It will get the person you're with to start doubting his or her influence over you and wondering if you're losing interest. It will motivate that person to become more attentive to your needs in an effort to maintain a hold on you. But this tactic requires fixed determination. Why? Because the unsettling effects of silence on a relationship can be as disturbing to you as it is to the one you're trying to win. The temptation for you to say something to break the silence and get the conversation going again can become almost overpowering. Wise is that person, who exercises self-discipline and resists this temptation, allowing the power of *silence* to work its disquieting miracle on the one they want. Those who learn to use this tactic appropriately will ultimately reap rich rewards from such an exercise of patience.

The nice thing about silence is that it leaves everything to the imagination of the other person. And when you're dealing with people's insecurities and self-doubts, imagination is always your best tool. *Telling* someone that he or she is in danger of losing you is not nearly as effective as letting that person *wonder.*

One young man named Jim, whose story is not at all uncommon, used this "silence" tactic with Shirley, the girl he later married. There was a time in their relationship when Shirley began taking his attention and tokens of affection for granted. Her respect for him was at a low point. One night when they were out together, Jim turned on the silent treatment as he was driving her home. This was quite a change from his usual outgoing self and, of course, she noticed it right away. As they drove along and the silence continued to build, the quiet completely undid her emotionally and shook her confidence. (That's what you have to do: *shake their confidence!*) For the first time in a long while she felt him slipping away, got quite humbled by it, and asked him to pull the car over. When he did so, Shirley told him with tears in her eyes that she had a feeling she was losing him, and asked if anything was wrong. She was ready to start making amends! Today they have been married for several decades.

This sort of reaction is not unusual, folks! It worked for one aspiring lover, and it will work for you, as well. Even if the one you want doesn't outwardly appear to be concerned about your silence, you can rest assured that, when done appropriately, this technique *will* cause them to secretly worry about losing you.

Another hopeful suitor, motivated by the above example, reported his attempts to use this same tactic on a pretty and popular girl who had begun acting somewhat aloof towards him. Even though he had managed to get her to agree to a date, she showed little enthusiasm once they were actually out. In fact, all evening long, she acted kind of bored and didn't contribute much to the conversation at all. Her attitude seemed to say, "Ho-hum, let's get this over with. I can't wait until he takes me home!"

Meanwhile, the young man pretended to be oblivious to her mood, and forced himself to remain talkative and friendly. Valiantly, he kept up his bravado, maintaining his enthusiasm throughout the evening in the face of her disrespectful attitude. It was obvious that she felt she had him wrapped around her finger, so her behavior remained like that of a spoiled child. However, she didn't know that her suitor had some understanding of the psychology of love, and actually had a plan in mind.

About ten or fifteen minutes before dropping her off, the young man abruptly changed his demeanor. Whereas every minute of the evening until then, he had been entirely devoted to her every whim and desire, he suddenly and totally stopped paying attention to her. He stopped smiling at her. He even stopped looking at her. And he *completely* stopped talking to her. He just kept his hands on the steering wheel and his eyes on the road ahead. It seemed as though his thoughts were suddenly a million miles away. He appeared totally preoccupied and aloof!

He knew *exactly* what he was doing, but she had no idea! This was certainly a stark contrast to the attentiveness he had exhibited to her throughout the earlier part of the evening. The silence was deafening. After a few minutes of his sudden change in behavior, the thought crossed her mind that, uh-oh, she might have offended him. (In fact, that's exactly what she had been unconsciously trying to do—brush him off without making herself appear like the bad guy.) Even though she had wanted to discourage him, she certainly didn't want him to be angry or think badly of her. She still wanted his admiration, and suddenly began working towards getting it back. So for the first time that night, *she* tried to pick up the conversation herself, but he responded with only curt though polite answers. He made no efforts to carry the conversation, as he had previously. In short, he was giving her back some of what she had been giving him all evening, and it was beginning to unnerve her.

At first, this love tactician planned to just drop her off without any further conversation at all. He wanted to leave her wondering what had happened. But then the most amazing thing occurred. She absolutely came *alive* in her efforts to revitalize his interest in her. Enthusiastically, she made a number of efforts to re-engage him in conversation. Furthermore, she started throwing all sorts of compliments his way, including commenting on what a wonderful evening she had been having. Meanwhile, amazed himself at the degree of his own success, the undeterred strategist continued to be polite but didn't encourage her. And then, when he still didn't seem to be won over, our now repentant object of pursuit tried feverishly to convince him to come in for a while. Although he went in, he stayed only a few minutes. This young man thoroughly understood the principle of playing hard to get, and it was working.

In an otherwise unlikely turn of events, this young lady's interest was greatly intensified. (You see, love tactics really do work!) From that point on, the attitude she exhibited toward him was appreciative and respectful. Don't be afraid to use the silent treatment when it's appropriate. If you don't pull in your welcome mat once in a while, eventually you'll be completely taken for granted. And that would be *fatal* to your hopes of inducing the one you want to feel any romantic interest in you.

So, occasionally turn on the silence—yes, let it get good and loud! If you have the courage to let the one you want go home at night with the echo of silence still ringing in his or her ears, it will, ironically, stimulate passion and stoke the fires of emotional desire for you!

36 Drop 'em Cold!

Nothing—absolutely nothing—can turn a person's disinterested, uncaring attitude around and make them burn with romantic desire for you like being dumped! Marital therapists have long been aware of this predictable reaction in human relationships. It is absolutely universal in its application. Apathetic feelings will typically turn into passionate longing when people realize that a possession they have taken for granted is in danger of being permanently lost.

A classic illustration of this is seen in the relationship between Rhett Butler and Scarlet O'Hara in *Gone With the Wind*. For most of the story, Rhett remains selflessly devoted to Scarlet and determined in his pursuit to win her love. However, she continuously takes him for granted. It's only when he walks out on her in the end and delivers his famous line, "Frankly, my dear, I don't give a damn," that Scarlet finally realizes she can't live without him.

The outcome of this situation is more true to life than most people realize. Consider this similar incident that happened to a college coed we will call Sandy. One of her admirers, a guy we'll call Mike, began pursuing Sandy with a passion. He showered her with phone calls, drop-in visits, and other bits of attention. But Sandy wasn't interested in Mike, and admitted feeling kind of annoyed and irritated by his interest in her. But in spite of her many brush-offs, Mike hung in there. He was persistent and showed he cared.

Finally, Sandy got what she wanted—or at least what she *thought* she wanted—and Mike suddenly gave up on her. He abruptly stopped coming around and calling. And would you like to guess what happened? Sandy admitted, "I actually started missing him."

You see, although neither of them realized it at the time, the attention and love Mike had been selflessly bestowing on Sandy had been successfully cultivating a subconscious bond of affection between them. But it was only when Mike dropped her that Sandy recognized her feelings and became aware of the fondness she had developed for him.

This type of reaction is not uncommon. *It is the rule!* In many cases, though, this unforeseen advantage to the suitor is lost. Why? Because the "dumper" never returns to the "dumpee" to pick up where they left off. By making a second effort, the dumper would find a much more responsive and appreciative dumpee, who would be eager for a second chance.

Every good salesman knows that in order to get a customer to buy, there has to be an element of urgency in the buyer's mind. There can never be a message from the salesman that implies, "Whenever you get around to it, everything you want will still be here waiting for you." Rather, a savvy salesman will urge the customer with a phrase like, "If you don't buy today, you may not have the opportunity tomorrow!" The psychology of selling is especially operative in romance, because, after all, the exchange of marriage vows is the most important sales transaction a person can ever make! The message you have to convey to the one you want is, "It's now or never!" And you have to reinforce the impact of this message by letting the person experience a little bit of what life can be like without you.

One couple had been going out for years, but the guy, whose name was Monty, had a non-committal attitude that prevented their relationship from progressing beyond a certain point. Tired of being taken for granted, the woman, now changed and self-respecting, informed her comfortable lover that she had been offered a job in another city and was moving. Monty, who never thought she had the intestinal fortitude to ever leave him, was shocked. He asked how she could even think of doing such a thing. She responded by saying, "I love you, Monty, but I can do fine without you." Well, that completely undid him (just as he deserved to be undone), and he proposed one week later! But if this woman of dignity hadn't shown her willingness to drop him cold and go on her merry way, their relationship would probably still be in limbo to this very day.

Just remember—most people aren't even aware of their addictions until the "supply" has been cut off. If you never let the one you want experience the pain of withdrawal by losing you for a while, they may never become fully aware of just how hooked they are on you! Wouldn't it be a shame to spend your entire life always being taken for granted by the one you want? Often, one good demonstration of emotional muscle flexing is all that is needed! Just showing how painful life can be without you will forever keep the one you want appreciative and respectful of you.

Some people claim that such tactics are exploitive and immoral. Not true! Yes, whenever you strive to enhance your own situation through the impairment of someone else's, you are being exploitive. But when you attempt to improve someone else's position *along with* your own, then that is good business—a win-win situation! Ideally, *both* parties in any human exchange or transaction should benefit, and that is certainly the aim of this book.

With this in mind, be bold and courageous! After you have been persistently selfless in a relationship, don't be afraid to drop 'em cold. Let the one you want experience what it's like to live without you for a while. Then magnanimously return and give them another chance. You'll be surprised at how effectively this tactic works!

37 *Create Competition*

Would you like to stir up the latent passions of the person you want and get them to actually *crave* your affections? Then create a challenge for them. Give your special someone something to be jealous of. Don't let them think they're the only show in town! Maintain friendships with those of the opposite sex. Go out and spend some time with them socially. Don't be afraid to flirt a little, either. It's absolutely amazing just how much a little rivalry can stir up a person's hot-blooded romantic desires for you!

One young man had been dating a girl somewhat casually for four years. But when he suddenly discovered that she had started dating someone else, he began to experience passionate feelings that he didn't even realize he had. Both his appreciation and affection for her were elevated to new heights!

Similarly, picture the one you want as a bomb filled with passionate feelings just waiting to be set off. All you have to do is light the fuse! Ann Landers once defined love as "friendship that has caught fire!" If this is so, then the key to love (once you have established a good, solid friendship) is simply to create some combustion! Competition can create the necessary spark!

The tactic of using rivalry to stir up passion is as old as romance itself. The ancient Roman poet Ovid wrote a number of works on the subject of love nearly two thousand years ago. In them, he strongly recommended the use of rivalry to stir up the reciprocated affections of the one you want! (It seems that no one—not even the stoic ancient Romans—has ever been immune to the frustrations brought on by affairs of the heart.)

But in spite of people's awareness of how well this rivalry technique works, many refrain from ever using it. Their reasoning is simple: They've narrowed down their interests to one person, so why waste their time on others? There are two very good reasons, though, to keep yourself in circulation. First, if you're to be fully appreciated by the one you want, *then he or she will have to feel lucky to get you.* It is, therefore, necessary to create the illusion that your affections could be lost to someone else. As the one you want becomes convinced of this possibility, their appreciation of you will soar. Second, as you interact with others (dating, just being friends, flirting, or whatever), your own emotional need for companionship will be somewhat satisfied. This will make you a stronger and more confident person in other aspects of your life, including your relationship with the one you want! In turn, this will help you to radiate a spirit of confidence and independence, further challenging your special person to new emotional heights. So don't become a hermit! Play the field! It's good for you *and* for the one you want!

38 *Break a Date!*

Although breaking a date with someone runs the risk of an angry reaction, this is precisely why it can be such an effective tool in winning that person's love! It shows that you're not intimidated by their opinion of you or what you do. It shows you do not fear their anger or potential rejection. It's a subtle way of reasserting yourself in a relationship at a time when the other person is beginning to think that he or she is "in control!" Breaking a date causes doubt in their ability to dominate you, which, in turn, will fan the flames of their romantic passion. Remember: People crave the unobtainable. They *most* desire to conquer that which appears invincible. Breaking a date can reestablish the challenge for the one you want, and create heightened interest and longing for you!

One guy discovered this truth after experiencing a number of romantic failures. He stated that he always tried to be open and honest with those he wanted, but found that his openness only drove them away. Time after time they would lose interest in him, always leaving him shortly after he confessed how much he cared. Finally, he figured out that it was this very openness that was destroying all of these good romantic possibilities. So he tried a new tactic. Instead of confessing devotion when a new relationship began to warm up, he called the girl on the phone and broke an approaching date.

Afterwards, he spent the night worrying (even *crying!*), thinking he had perhaps blown one of the best things ever to come along in his life. *But he didn't blow it!* Where others had deserted him at this particular stage in previous relationships, this girl fell madly in love with him! You see, he had maintained the challenge of romance for her and she had responded accordingly! So don't be afraid to use this tactic. It will work for you, too!

10

Keeping Them Interested and Hoping

Principle: *In order to keep a person romantically interested in you, he or she must have some hope that you will reciprocate their interest.*

---

*R*omantic infatuation is a delicately balanced human response that thrives on uncertainty. On the one hand, too much self-confidence will kill excitement. On the other hand, a lack of confidence will starve it to death. So while keeping the one you want from any certainty that you're hooked on them, you must still provide them with some glimmers of hope that you might become so! How do you do this? Read on.

39 *Pop Back into Their Life*

Once you have given the other person reason to think you are losing interest in the relationship, surprise him or her with a phone call or drop by unexpectedly. Most important, start going places and doing things together again.

Part of the overall strategy of this book is to keep the one you want somewhat confused and off balance. You don't want the person to know quite what to expect from you next! Your interest should appear to shift from hot to cold, and then back again. (You may have heard the expression, "blowing hot and cold." Well, it works like magic to mesmerize the one you want.) Any seasoned lover knows the importance of varying the approach while developing a relationship. This type of unpredictability is as essential to romantic survival as changing colors at will is to the survival of a chameleon.

As a general rule, people are more prone to respond when given a second chance with others. This is because they are much more motivated! Recipients of your love aren't able to fully appreciate how truly blessed they are to have your attentions until they've experienced the void that comes in its absence. Thus, when an opportunity to regain it comes along, there will be much greater appreciation and passionate desire. That's why, as Frank Sinatra sings it, "Love's more comfortable, the second time around." So after letting the one you want stew for a while, thinking they have lost you, resume contact and *give them that second chance!*

Just because the going gets tough does not mean that the relationship is over. It's not over until you quit. So don't be afraid to take a tough stand from time to time, to scold if necessary, or even to break off contact with the one you want. Just be sure to resume contact and pick up where you left off after the smoke clears. You'll be surprised at how positive the results will be!

40 *Send Mementos*

After (and *only* after) you've created some uncertainty on the part of the one you want regarding your feelings toward them, you may send a small memento of your affection to revive their hopes. It could be a short note or a small gift—just make sure your communication is vague and non-committal. Keep written communications to a minimum. The very fact that you are taking the time to send anything at all intrinsically sends the message that you care.

A word of caution. Don't send mementos too early in a relationship, or at a time when the other person is already feeling overconfident about your feelings. If this happens, any additional evidence of your caring will be taken for granted. The very person you are attempting to win could wind up disrespecting (and, even worse, despising) you. Yet this continues to be a common mistake of naïve lovers. Don't feed somebody else's already oversized ego! Remember that passion thrives on insecurity. Before you make a person's day by sending them a token of your affection, make sure that they are in the throes of doubt regarding whether you like them or not. If the one you want is not in actual agony over you, your tokens of thoughtfulness will only invoke pity or scorn. It is far better to refrain from this tactic until you are absolutely certain of their state of mind. You can't go guessing on this one.

41 *Awaken Physical Attraction*

The exhilarating experience of "falling in love" is unquestionably a sex-linked phenomenon. Whether you're conscious of it or not, the mainspring of all romantic activities is the instinctive sexual drive of the human species. Its constancy and strength is what keeps husbands and wives and, consequently, families together in the first place. Without it, few people would be sufficiently motivated to commit their lives to another individual in such an exclusive arrangement as that of marriage.

For this reason, it is futile to expect to win someone's heart completely and fully without being able to stir up some physical desire for you. And that, dear friend, is why kissing was invented! Serving as much to stir up passions as to gratify them, kissing is an invaluable tool for helping to bond couples emotionally and prepare them for marriage. The kiss provides a subtle incentive for increased physical closeness. It is a tool (much like fire) with a similar potential for good or bad, through proper or improper use. If used wisely, the fires that are awakened can motivate people to make the commitments necessary for permanent relationships. But if allowed to burn out of control, they can destroy any hope of permanency in a relationship.

"That's just fine," you might say, "if you can get the person to kiss you in the first place! But how do you get over *that* hurdle?" No problem. The underlying philosophy of *Love Tactics* is that a person must *act,* not *react,* in order to succeed at romance. So when the other person shows no inclination to initiate affection, *you* must be the aggressive one. It doesn't matter if you're male or female, as long as you've already established a firm foundation based on friendship and respect before making your move. It doesn't matter who takes the first step, as long as *somebody* does.

Make sure the one you want is comfortable with your physical closeness by engaging in non-sexual contact first. Everyone desires the warmth of physical affection and human touch. Sometimes, however, the person you want may be uncomfortable in either expressing *or* receiving physical affection. Why? Often it is because the person is just not accustomed to close physical contact. In such cases, you have to gradually "condition" a person to be touched by you. How? By proceeding very patiently. Begin by touching the person you are with in a brief, non-sexual way. When engaged in conversation, occasionally make some sort of physical contact—generally, a person's back, shoulders, and arms can be touched with little risk of a traumatic response. Perhaps guide your date through the door of a restaurant by putting a non-threatening arm around her back. Take her hand to help her out of the car. Give him a playful nudge while taking a stroll through the park. You get the idea.

Eventually, however, you must move on to the real thing. When you finally *do* sense that the time is right for that kiss, don't be timid about it. Don't seem like you intend to "test the waters" first, one toe at a time. Just go for it! Act as though you've made an independent decision about what you want to do. Act as if it's irrelevant to you whether the person has any desire to kiss you back or not. Make it seem almost as though it's just a game to you—a lark or a challenge—and that it's no big deal if the person isn't interested in kissing you back. (By the way, the first kisses are probably better if they're short and sweet. A long, passionate, suffocated kiss right away may result in a short, impassionate, suffocated relationship. Make it a *fun* thing, rather than a *serious* event.)

What happens when the one you want does *not,* in fact, want to kiss you back? That's no big problem either. It's okay. Don't let it throw you. Haven't you ever heard of "stealing" a kiss? *Trying* to kiss the person is part of the process of warming them up and instilling the desire! Remember—success in romance (or in any other project in life, for that matter) is dependent on your willingness to *act* independently of other people's opinions, and not merely to *react*. *Love Tactics* is not merely a system of guidelines to analyze people and figure out whether their whim of the moment is to *like* you or not. Rather, it's an active system of principles to help you *win their love*, whether they like you at first or not!

What happens if the one you want turns away from your initial kissing overtures? Just carry on with normal conversation as if nothing happened. Ignore any rebuff as if it's no big deal. Later on, in the quiet hours of reflective contemplation *after* the date, the seeds of desire will begin to grow. The one you want will begin to wonder, to fantasize about what it might have been like *if* . . . and the next time it will happen!

When your kiss is returned, kiss with enthusiasm, but not for *too* long! *You* should be the one to end the kiss. It's better to leave the person hungering for more, rather than bored by too much! Why? Because if you continue kissing for so long that the other person feels the need to terminate the experience, you'll diminish your influence in the future. Remember: *You* should be the one to initiate the kiss, and *you* should be the one to say when enough is enough. Maintain control. It will drive the one you want wild!

As for more passionate physical intimacies, you'll find them contrary to the focus of this book. It is strongly advised to avoid them altogether until you are married. This may not be what you want to hear, but past experience only confirms the wisdom of this counsel. Historically speaking, people in nations with strict codes of morality and chastity have been happier. Those who await the marriage chamber to consummate their love are more serious about their commitments to one another, and have a more stable family life. The more intimate physical privileges that are traditionally reserved for marriage are, in fact, the very *enticements* of marriage itself! To engage in them prematurely and, in effect, give away your bargaining chips only diminishes your own worth to the other person, and can destroy any chances of developing a real sense of commitment in the relationship. *Somebody* is going to be used, and there will not be enough respect to cultivate the full and complete romantic love necessary to the happiness of both parties. Frequently, however, couples indulge in such mutual exploitation without realizing the damage they are doing to the relationship.

And make no mistake about it—the ultimate goal of *Love Tactics* all along has been to convince the one you want to marry you! The most rewarding love of all is that which exists *in the institution of marriage!* But if you surrender your body and soul in full measure to another person prematurely, without first entering into the marriage covenant, you will unwittingly sabotage your efforts to attain this objective.

Sure, premarital sex runs rampant in today's society. But look around you. Isn't *unfulfilled love* just as prevalent? You see, it's not that premarital sex is harmful because it's disapproved. Rather, it's disapproved because it's harmful! It spells the difference between a temporary relationship and a *lasting* one, between superficial caring and committed love.

We will, however, stand by our recommendation to use kissing to enhance a relationship, reminding you to maintain control at all times. The prudent use of kissing will help you to secure a commitment and win lasting love from the one you want.

11

Confronting Diplomatically

Principle: *When the one you want feels that you really understand and accept them, their ability to resist loving you will go out the window. No logic will be able to prevent them from falling in love with you.*

One of the most challenging obstacles you will encounter in your pursuit of the one you want is their tentative assessment that you can't handle the truth about them. They'll suspect that if you know who they really are inside, or how they truly feel about you, you will judge and reject them. They'll fear that if the whole truth were to come out, they will lose your respect and friendship. They'll think, for example, that it would just about kill you if they were to admit they're not romantically attracted to you. They also believe that once the cat's out of the bag, you won't continue thinking highly of them anymore. So, trying to be kind and to continue being well thought of, the person will hide the truth and look for some way out of the relationship without having to disclose the real reasons.

However, if you allow the one you want to avoid confronting you with the truth, it is *this very allowance* that is likely to be the coup de grâce to the relationship. Letting them get their cards out on the table will ultimately save the relationship. Truth is what sets you both free. Suppression of the truth impedes the growth of love. You must make it clear that you are able to face the truth (even if it means romantic rejection), and that you can accept it without being shattered. The psychological secret here is that when you show the strength to face their rejection and not fall apart or become bitter, they will begin to change their mind. Their subconscious does a flip-flop, and they begin to see you through new eyes. They begin to realize that you've known all along where you stand with them, and that you sincerely care for them anyway.

When people feel that deep down you don't understand their doubts and fears, then they conclude you really don't know and accept them for who they truly are. If they believe that you would be crushed and embittered upon discovering their real feelings for you, then they will also conclude that your love for them is shallow and conditional. They will conclude that your admiration is based upon some fantasy version of the person you merely *think* they are. Of course, they won't want to let the truth out and have you hate them.

Miraculously, though, as soon as you demonstrate that you can both sense their true feelings *and* accept them, even in the face of your own personal rejection, their very doubts and objections will become unimportant to them. When faced with the realization that, "My goodness! Here's a person who *really* cares about me in spite of myself!" their other reasons for hesitation towards you will pale in comparison with the prospect of being truly loved for *who they are!* And when a person feels truly understood, accepted, and, yes, loved, somehow concerns that once seemed so important, won't mean as much anymore. When someone realizes you love them to the core, they cannot help but fall in love with you, in spite of all the reasons they can think of why they shouldn't. In the final analysis, after all, love is truly a language of the emotions —not logic!

42 Confront Resistant Behavior

As you attempt to develop a relationship with someone, quite often that person will begin to experience doubts about what he or she is getting into, and develop some extremely logical, personally convincing, *secret* reasons why the relationship is all wrong. Hesitating to get into the relationship any deeper, he or she will begin to show distinct signs of resistant behavior towards you. This resistance manifests itself in various symptoms, including moody behavior, guarded and unresponsive communication, disrespect, and, finally, outright avoidance of you.

Such behavior must be confronted. If these underlying feelings of doubt remain buried, they will ultimately destroy the relationship. We have found the CARE method to be most effective in preventing such destruction. It is based on four steps—Confronting, Asking, Reassuring, and Empathizing:

1. **Confront** the person's uncooperative behavior. "Maybe I'm mistaken, but I sense that something's wrong . . ." One of the most exhilarating experiences a person can have in life is the feeling of being understood. We don't want to have to *tell* others when we are feeling distraught. We want them to sense it on their own. We want them to read our minds. As one frustrated wife tried to explain, as she was in the process of divorcing her oblivious husband, "What spouses want in a companion is someone who can read them like a book." Subconsciously, people give clues as to what they're thinking by their actions. Ignoring those clues is a prescription for disaster. Many people live in denial regarding what's going on in a relationship because they're afraid of what they might learn. But being sensitive to such unspoken acts through confrontation will go a long way towards satisfying your loved one's need for understanding. This, in turn, will help eliminate emotional obstacles to their commitment and love for you.

2. **Ask** for a confirmation or denial of your observations. "Am I reading you right?" "Is something actually bothering you?" By letting people know the message that their unspoken behavior is communicating to you, and then asking for a validation of your interpretation, you will help them analyze their own subconscious intentions. "Hmm . . . I *have* been acting rather cold and distant . . . Why? What exactly do I mean by this behavior? What have I been trying to communicate here?"

Through your questions, you will help others become consciously aware of what is motivating their actions toward you. They have been intimating something all along that they subconsciously wish they could say aloud to you, but have been afraid to. All you're doing is helping them to say what's on their mind. Through your assistance, they'll be able to crystallize their feelings through verbalization. People often behave in certain ways without really knowing why. The first step in changing their attitude is to get them to recognize *for themselves* what that attitude is. And it doesn't really matter if they're ready to come clean and openly admit their feelings or not. The mere realization that you have *already* been listening to them *with your heart,* and are willing to listen more, will go a long way in stripping away their resistance. In the long run, logic cannot withstand the force of emotion. Feeling understood and accepted by you will ultimately override any previous hesitation they may have felt about surrendering their heart to you.

Don't push for more details than necessary. You don't have to. You have already helped them more than you can imagine just by opening their mind. You have lifted them to a point where they can decide for themselves where they now want to go. They will have been brought to a crossroads where they have to choose between honesty and repentance. If they choose honesty, they'll admit what's been troubling them. But if not, then they'll have to change their old attitude and let go of their concerns. Either choice is good for the relationship.

3. *Reassure* the person of your intention to merely understand—not judge—on the basis of what is admitted, especially if he or she seems a little hesitant to express those feelings. Use terms like, "If you're willing to talk, I'm willing to just listen. I just care about how you feel." One major reason for breakdowns in communication is the fear of being judged. Human experience has conditioned most people to expect others to respond to their honest feelings with judgment and criticism. Some encouragement from you will be necessary to assure the one you want that he or she will not be thought less of because of personal fears or concerns.

4. *Empathize.* Be understanding. Once the person starts to open up a little, just listen like you promised you would. Don't blow it! Don't criticize or try to change the person's mind or show how flawed their reasoning is. If you do, you'll regret it, because he or she will probably not open up to you again (or at least for a very long time). Instead, let the person proceed at a comfortable pace. Show signs of reflective listening by nodding your head and gently encouraging the person to continue by using terms like, "Mm-hmmm" and "Yes, go on." Just *don't* pronounce judgment on what is being said! Of course, the acid test will come when the one you want admits to having doubts about the relationship. Don't panic when he or she states the two of you are not right for each other! Remain calm, no matter how rejected you feel! *You are still going to win out!*

First, though, you must defuse such sentiments by allowing the person to get those feelings out in the open. Then you must resist the urge to try to change their mind. You must be *completely accepting* of them. Showing that you disagree will only reinforce their feelings of doubt. (Although this may not seem to make sense, it's how it really works!) Once you have shown that you are totally accepting of the person's feelings at the time of the discussion, stop calling or stopping by for several days. This will give them a sense of relief and of being truly understood. Then initiate contact again without warning and in a platonic way; just be a friend. In this way, you will convey your intentions to maintain the friendship, even without the romance. You may rest assured that romance will come along in due time. By doing this, you will have made it possible to rekindle that romance in the future.

Your willingness to let the one you want open up to you at a comfortable pace, coupled with your obvious sensitivity to what is bothering him or her, will encourage greater reliance on you. This method of understanding is one of the finest ways to communicate love, and to overcome any obstacles that may be blocking your romantic progress.

12

Demonstrating Commitment

Principle: *The more someone is convinced of his or her personal importance to you, the more intense will be their feelings of love.*

---

*A*fter all is said and done, the ever-present question of both participants in a relationship is, "How important am I to you *really?*" All other questions are mere offshoots of this one. The more valued each feels to the other, the greater will be their feelings of love in return. The following tactics illustrate how you can successfully instill this feeling of importance in the one you want.

43 *Hang in There!*

Occasionally after all is said and done, it will appear that the one you want is completely unmoved by your efforts. *But don't be fooled by such deceptive appearances!* This is simply nature's way of shaking out those pursuers who are less sincere—and less committed. Your challenge is to prove through endurance that your love is *true*. However, in your frustration, you may find yourself asking, "What am I doing wrong?" If you've done your best to apply the tactics in this book faithfully, the answer is, "Nothing." You are on the right track. Keep using the tactics—your skill will improve with practice as you learn from your mistakes. In time, reciprocation will come.

By the way, you're allowed to make mistakes! It's okay if your voice shakes occasionally, or you fall flat on your face every now and then. You're only human, and people will still love you in spite of these things—maybe even *because* of them. Just keep getting back up and trying again. The only permanent mistake you can really make is to quit.

If you have had a handful of dates with a particular person and still feel like you're not making any progress, don't be discouraged. An article that was written by psychologist Dr. Joyce Brothers should encourage every hopeful but frustrated lover. Commenting on a survey of married couples, she disclosed that over half of the women interviewed said they didn't feel that they were in love with their husbands-to-be until after at least twenty dates! In other words, it's possible to *grow* to love someone. Men, as well, grow to love those women who patiently continue to interact with them.

THE VALLEY OF THE SHADOW OF APATHY

How well can you hang in there? This depends on your ability to persevere even when you occasionally lose feelings of desire. In other words, there will come a time when all the excitement you first felt for this special person will temporarily dissipate. Expect it! You may find yourself thinking, "Wow! There was a time when all the effort seemed worth it. But now I feel like I don't even care anymore! Before, it seemed like the one I wanted was worth *any* price. But now I'm not sure I'd want that person even if he or she came begging!"

This, too, shall pass. You're actually closer than ever to your goal. *Now* is the time when your true ability to love will be tried. This is because love in its ultimate form is a commitment of pure will power—with no gratification attached. This doesn't mean that you don't deserve happiness and emotional fulfillment anymore. You *do*, and it will still happen. But first you must walk through the valley of the shadow of "apathy" to claim your prize! Be forewarned that this experience is inevitable in any developing, worthwhile relationship.

Is it reasonable to ask you to hang in there forever, with no desire or hope of gratification ever again? Of course not! But if you hang in there for a while, in spite of any temporary loss of interest, your feelings of desire will eventually return. If you're truly committed to endure to the end, there is no heart that you won't be able to win over. To quote a well-known maxim, "The race is not to the swift, nor the battle to the strong, but to him that endureth to the end."

At times, it may seem awfully frustrating and you may not know all the answers, but rest assured, there *are* answers. There *are* solutions. There *is* a way. It's just a matter of persisting until you find out what that way is. You can do it!

44 Say "I Love You"

Although earlier in this book we stated that you shouldn't wear your heart on your sleeve, there does come a time in a relationship when it is appropriate to say, "I love you." But this time comes only after you have consistently proven your love—not with *words*, but with *actions*. Words are cheap, and people know it. Remember: "What you do screams so loudly in my ears, I can't hear a single word you say!"

The main thing to remember when expressing your love is that people tend to run from commitments. If someone suspects by your words that what you are really saying is, "I want a commitment from you," it may inadvertently drive that person away. Use the words "I love you," but try to do so while also conveying the message that, "It doesn't matter whether you return my affections or not. My desire for your happiness stands, regardless!" The degree to which the one you want actually believes this will determine your success in winning his or her love. Your words must somehow convey that your love is an unconditional commitment with no strings attached. It mustn't come across as an attempt to back the person into a corner where he or she will feel obligated to say "I love you" in return. People will *not* allow themselves to be trapped this way. Expect much, gain little. Expect little, gain much!

Remember, these three little words can lose their potency if your actions contradict them. Think of the words "I love you" as the bullet, and your actions as the gunpowder. If you put a bullet in your musket without having packed in a good supply of gunpowder first, it will fall harmlessly to the ground when you fire your weapon. On the other hand, if you forget to load the bullet, even though you have packed in a good supply of gunpowder, your firearm will be just as ineffective.

When America became a new nation, its position was a fragile one. It didn't have the expertise or strength of the British Forces, nor did it possess the financial resources of England. Colonel William Prescott, who led the American troops at the Battle of Bunker Hill, realized the precariousness of his untrained army's position against the stronger English forces. Upon observing the enemy's advancement up the hill, he advised his men, "Don't shoot until you see the whites of their eyes!" He knew that they might never get a second chance, so their first shots had to count. Likewise, when you're trying to win the one you want, realize that there will be only so many opportunities to effectively say, "I love you." So don't say it too soon, or the words won't have any real force behind them.

Patiently prove your love first. Keep watching the one you want advance steadily "up the hill to the slaughter." Then, when you can see "the whites of their eyes" and sense that the timing of your words will have the proper impact, *fire away!* If you imagine that you've got only one shot and have to make it count, intuitively, you will be more capable of choosing the right moment to say, "I love you!"

.

13

Removing Final Barriers

Principle: *By backing off from a relationship that you have been aggressively pursuing for some time, the other person will automatically let down his or her emotional guard and, thus, become more vulnerable to your renewed advances in the future.*

Often, when people continue to resist you, it is because they think you haven't gotten the message yet. Of course, they realize that you are aware of their *declared* intentions to stay uninvolved and uncommitted to you; but they think you don't really realize how serious they are.

Backing off from the relationship for a while can take care of all that! At this point, you have to convince the person that you really understand that he or she means business about not wanting to get involved with you. And staying away is the only effective way to convince that individual that you understand. If you can succeed at this communication, within a short period of time, you will be able to turn the tables on their attitude. Once you've shown your ability to understand, you'll be on much firmer ground to stage your comeback.

45 *Strategically Withdraw*

Among the famous legends of ancient Greece is the story of the Tro-

123

jan Horse. For ten long, frustrating years the Greeks had assaulted the city of Troy in an unsuccessful attempt to win back their beautiful queen, Helen. The walls of the city were impenetrable, though, and the Greeks found it impossible to get inside. Direct confrontation appeared hopeless. Finally, they resorted to a much more subtle strategy, which proved to be most effective. They built a large wooden horse, and hid some of their soldiers inside. They left the horse just outside the walls of Troy, while the rest of the army boarded ships and began to sail away in what appeared to be a sign of retreat. Thinking the Greeks had given up, the Trojans opened their gates for the first time in years. Upon discovering the horse, they were fascinated by it. No longer feeling threatened by a direct confrontation with the Greek army, the Trojans let down their guard. Viewing the horse as spoils of their "victory," the Trojans brought it into the heart of the city.

That night, while the Trojans slept, the Greek soldiers slipped out of the horse and opened the gates of the city to their comrades who had sailed back in the dark of night and were waiting outside the gates. Troy was destroyed and Helen was saved. Strategic withdrawal had accomplished in a single day what ten years of direct encounter had failed to achieve.

Likewise, after aggressively pursuing the one you want and finding the stony walls around their heart to be unyielding to your love, employ the Trojan Horse technique by making a strategic withdrawal. The sense of relief that most people will experience by letting down their emotional guard will be great. This sets the stage for a victorious comeback. When faced with your eventual return, the one you want will not be willing—or able—to resist.

The great lesson of the Trojan Horse is this: Things that cannot be accomplished by pure force can often be accomplished through strategy. Love is not something that can be forced; but by using persuasive strategies that are based on sound behavioral principles, it *can* be cultivated!

46 *Enjoy Being with the One You Want!*

After all is said and done, love ends where it begins—with commitment. The ultimate objective is to win someone who is truly committed to you and to your happiness. However, it all begins with your commitment to that person.

The reason so many romantic relationships don't work out is because neither person involved in the relationship is ever truly committed to the other's acceptance and happiness *unconditionally*. Each one expects the other to demonstrate commitment first. But when someone becomes aware of your unconditional love, that person will inevitably love you back. In the words of Ralph Waldo Emerson, "Love, and you shall be loved."

When you have accomplished all that you've set out to do and finally win the one you want, enjoy! Nothing material can compare with being happily in love, so take the time to stop and appreciate what you have. Realize that love is worth more than all the treasures on earth. So, be aware of this fact, and quietly give thanks to divine Providence. Good luck, and enjoy being with the one you want!

PART TWO

Winning Back the One You've Lost

Many of our readers write to us about damaged or broken relationships—even marriages—and wonder if there are tactics that can help restore the love that once was there. Can former loves be won again? The answer is yes. But don't start jumping for joy yet. As you will see, it takes time and patience.

Nothing in life ever comes without a price. The harvest of love does not come spontaneously. It requires a time for planting and a time for cultivation. Where severe damage has occurred to a crop that once existed, time must be taken first to clear the field. Only then can one start to recultivate.

So the main difference between restoring a broken relationship and beginning a new one is that it may take longer to restore the broken one. Time is needed to undo weeks, months, or even years of damage that have taken their toll on the relationship. As we have already said, the only real mistake you can make is to quit trying.

Remember, part of the process of cultivating deep, lasting love normally includes going through rotten, difficult, insecure times. Wisely did Shakespeare say, "The course of true love never did run smooth." For some reason, rocky roads actually make relationships stronger once they have been successfully travelled together. People who withdraw from the challenge when the going gets rough never get to enjoy the fruits of accomplishing something truly wonderful.

Remember, when the going gets tough, the tough get going! It's worth going through some pain for things that are worthwhile. True love means *commitment*, and you must decide if you are really committed to making the relationship work. Don't think that just because you're going through some rough sailing you're doomed to sink. The trick is to fight to keep your ship on course.

As baseball great Yogi Berra said, "It's not over till it's over!" And in love, there's no umpire except you. It's not over until you say it's over. That gives you all the power. If the relationship has fallen apart, think about what went wrong. Reevaluate. Are there changes you can make? Are you willing to make those changes? Making positive changes will help you make personal progress in becoming a better person . . . someone more capable of giving and receiving love. There is no reason in the world why you should ever believe the one you've lost is lost forever. However, it may be easier to start over with someone new. Only *you* can decide whether it's worth it or not to try to fix a damaged relationship. *Love Tactics* gives you power through knowledge, but you must be practical and use common sense.

Although, ideally, you can win if you hang in there long enough, sometimes it's just not in your best interest to do so. Every decision in life ultimately comes down to this question: When should you keep trying, and when should you throw in the towel? Keep in mind the words of the famous Serenity Prayer: "God, grant me the serenity to accept the things I cannot change, the courage to change the things I can, and the wisdom to know the difference." A good guide to live by, this prayer is the motto of a growing army of empowered human beings in twelve-step groups around the world.

Yes, in time you can win almost anyone's heart by using the correct methods. But don't ever believe that you can really change the person! You may win a heart, but you'll never change its nature. You must *truly* be willing to ultimately accept the other person just as he or she is. If you are not very careful, you may win someone's love only to realize it does not bring the fulfillment for which you had hoped.

So be sure you want a person who is truly your best choice, rather than someone who is attractive because he or she is unobtainable. It's quite a decision, and one you must ultimately make by yourself.

14

Learning How to Win Back a Lost Love

Principle: *As long as life remains, there is still time to restore and constructively build a relationship.*

---

*P*erhaps you are thinking, "I wish I had read this book sooner. Is there any hope for me to win back the person I lost? Or is it now too late?" The answer is yes, there is always hope, and no, it is never too late. At this juncture, you simply must go back and start anew to apply the knowledge that is now in your hands. Don't be afraid of failure. Expect success from this moment on. Effective strategies for winning back the one you have lost are found throughout this book. You just need to apply them.

Like any skill, though, it takes practice to properly implement love strategies. Practice consists of trying and failing, trying again and failing a little less, trying more and getting the hang of it, and finally succeeding on a consistent basis. But none of this will happen unless you get out there, do your best, and refuse to give up.

47 Decide if It's Worth It

Since there will be an emotional cost associated with winning back the one you want, it makes no sense to throw good energy after bad unless you are committed to seeing the project through to the end. Whether you decide to try to salvage a previous relationship or to start out new with somebody else, both will require an extensive commitment of your time and effort. But in evaluating which course to take, we offer the following for your consideration:

■ **Objectively assess how much damage you've already done, and how much effort will be required to fix it.**
The first thing you need to do when determining how much damage you may have caused in your pre-existing relationship is to consider how seriously you violated the principles essential for nurturing love and for how long. A man we will call J.B. spent over ten years emotionally abusing his wife. She eventually hardened her heart toward him and left. The big shock for J.B. was that he hadn't seen it coming until the day she walked out on him. We were surprised that it took her so long.

Love can conceivably be restored in a relationship, even one in which abuse has occurred. But in J.B.'s case, it would take a long, long time, even if he straightened up his act and didn't make another mistake. The longer you neglect the rules of love, the longer it will take to fix the resulting failed relationship.

One of the major rules of medicine found in the Hippocratic Oath is "First, do no harm;" but in love and courtship, such wisdom is routinely ignored. It is possible to have done so much damage to a relationship that it will take more time to win that person back, than it will to start a new relationship from scratch. Only you can decide if you are patient enough to pay the price of your setback.

As you objectively review your past role in the relationship, consider the things you did right as well as the things you did wrong. For instance, how much time did you spend showing consideration and kindness by listening to your partner? How often were you attentive? Did you build up your companion with words of praise and appreciation? Were you generous with hugs and other nonsexual signs of physical affection?

On the other hand, were you critical or manipulative? How

often? Constantly, or only occasionally? Were you excessively permissive in the relationship? Did you allow yourself to be spoken to disrespectfully or treated with disdain? Did you insist, for the good of the relationship, that your own needs, as well as your partner's, be met? Were you a clinging vine? Were you whiny? Did you appear to be unequally dependent on your partner?

Each of these questions must be addressed objectively. Go through this book, tactic by tactic, if necessary, to help you accurately assess where you really stand. If, on average, you have built a solid foundation for love, it is possible that with some fine-tuning you might be able to turn the relationship around in a matter of days. Sometimes you can be much closer to winning back the one you want than either of you may realize. But if you have built a weak foundation by straying from the tried and true principles of love, the relationship is going to take extensive time to fix.

It is difficult to be brutally honest with yourself, but now is the time. Otherwise you could spend a lot of time spinning your wheels for nothing. You can win the one you want, but you have to know what you're up against.

You need to ask yourself some hard questions, such as the ones above, and be honest with your answers. Often we find ourselves in the middle of problems because we have been in denial for so long. Furthermore, it is likely that the one you want may have actually brought up the problem (or problems) long ago, but through stubbornness, you refused to accept it. Ask yourself if it is possible that you were given clues, but refused to recognize them.

Another part of this assessment process involves determining how much effort will be needed on your part to restore the relationship. Just because you know what to do doesn't necessarily mean you have the intestinal fortitude to pull it off successfully! There is no sense wasting your time hoping to salvage a relationship if you're not willing to make the necessary personal adjustments yourself. If you're not willing to change, don't bother wasting everyone's time, because you'll just run into the same old problems. If you want the same results, keep doing the same thing. But if you want a better outcome, it's up to you to make it better.

You don't have to be perfect, but you do have to be growing and improving. Even though you may have high ideals, understand that absolute perfection will elude you. Still, you should try to be as perfect as you can. You may not hit the bull's eye, but by aiming at it, you will continuously improve and get closer and closer. And in most cases, a sincere effort is sufficient to win back the one you want.

■ **Determine if restoring the relationship is worth the effort.**
Once you realize the price that must be paid in order to win back your lost love, a question must be faced. Are you willing to pay that price, whatever it may be? Are you willing to endure without reward for as long as it may take? If so, then this is an undertaking that's worth the effort. Prepare to bite the bullet! In the end, though, your sacrifice will pay off.

However, if you find yourself simply wanting to reestablish the relationship quickly, but are not willing to spend the necessary time to repair the damaged ties, then wake up and face the real world! You're wasting your time if you're hoping that things will fix themselves. Acknowledge that, in this case, the price is just too great. Write off the relationship to experience and look for another. But remember that if you repeat the same mistakes in a fresh relationship and don't make changes in your own attitudes, this relationship will be destined for failure as well. None of us can escape the need to change for the better.

■ **Know how to let go.**
If you decide the relationship has ended and there is no possibility of reconciliation (for whatever reason), you may still have to face another problem. Although logically you know you must give up someone up, emotionally you may have a difficult time doing so. It's not that you're *unwilling* to give up the person, it's that you just can't seem to do it!

Here's some good news. Time really does heal all wounds. And time can help you even more effectively if you help it along. Keep your mind occupied. Get involved in worthwhile activities while you come to grips with your loss. Diverting your mind can relieve a lot of the pain and restore your emotional strength.

A young woman who had been through several broken relationships shared her prescription for getting over a heartache. She called it her Get-a-New-Dog Theory. If you lose a pet, some people believe it will help if you get another. In some ways, relationships with people are similar. True, you may never totally forget or replace the one you've lost. But getting a substitute can help. Just realize that substitutes don't last forever, and you're not going to be completely fulfilled until the replacement becomes permanent. This, of course, is done by correctly applying the principles of love and romance.

We warn you against hasty, ill-considered rebounding. Make sure the replacement for your lost love has as many desirable qualities as possible. Take your time narrowing the field. When you choose wisely, selecting someone who is capable of meeting your emotional needs for love, you'll be surprised how healed and comforted you can still feel in spite of an earlier loss.

48 *Know When to "Cut Your Losses"*

Any person's heart can be won eventually, since every human heart responds to being loved. However, some hearts are not worth the time it takes to win them. There are often many other opportunities that may be better for you.

Does it make sense to spend years cultivating a harvest in barren ground, when a more fertile field lies just next door? (And often it does!) Does it make sense to spend years walking on eggshells, having to watch every word you say, when you could be enjoying those years with a person who nurtures and comforts *you?*

Although it is human to want the prize that is difficult to win, don't be baited into wanting someone solely because he or she is not available! Remember, you have to continue living with this person once you have won them over. However, you wouldn't be the first victim of the delusions of passionate desire if you chose unwisely on this basis. Many souls realize after a lifetime of misery that the only reason they ever wanted the one they wound up with was because he or she was hard to get! Once they got that person, they eventually realized the reality didn't meet up to the ideal. Instead of considering the unselfish and giving qualities of a love prospect, they thought only of how unavailable that person was. Some basic personality traits don't change. Be cautious of wanting someone who isn't considerate and kind, or one who is a "taker" 100-percent of the time.

On the other hand, beware of getting involved with neurotic people-pleasers, who go overboard in their attentiveness toward others. This "giving" personality type can actually smother you, quenching your flames of desire. Be careful not to jump into a committed relationship with this type of person either.

So choose the one you want wisely. It could be that by having lost the one you want, Nature is giving you another chance to exercise prudence and discretion in your final selection. Don't throw away such an opportunity.

15

Showing a Willingness to Change

Principle: *The better you are as a person, the more irresistible you become.*

---

*L*et's assume that you are not giving up on the relationship. You want to give it one more concerted try. Let's discuss some of the strategies that can help you.

One of the most essential attitudes necessary in applying the suggestions in *Love Tactics* is to realize that no one is perfect. However, you should be working to progress as much as you can towards perfection.

Understand that change is a lifelong process. As you learn the lessons life has to teach you, you should apply those lessons by showing a willingness to change and improve. This requires humility. It requires recognizing that you're not perfect. It requires acknowledging faults.

But take comfort. There is no such thing as a person without faults. If you learn the lessons life has for you, and make the changes necessary to apply those lessons in the future, you'll ultimately come out on top. Recognize that you *can* make changes, and that those changes can help you become a better and happier person.

49 *Assess Your Strengths and Weaknesses*

It is helpful to understand that, presently, the one you have lost may feel that you are not the person of their dreams. That's all right. It's okay to be imperfect. It's okay to be resistible. It does not necessarily mean that you have permanently lost that person. You can still work your way back into his or her heart. You must, though, be honest and willing to change. Recognize your strengths and weaknesses. When you face a weakness, acknowledge it, then accept it. (Ironically, this will transform that weakness into a strength!) By going through this process, you'll *become* the desirable person your loved one once perceived you to be, only this time, it won't be just an illusion.

How can you use this process to help you win back the one you have lost? Remember that any time you face the truth and acknowledge your own weaknesses, you have already taken a big step forward to becoming a better person, and it will show outwardly. There's a certain inner strength that comes with accepting reality instead of living in denial about who you are. People will sense this humility and tend to admire it, often overlooking other deficiencies you may have. It is the complete opposite for the insecure braggart who lives in a fantasy world of his own making. People tend to disrespect such a person.

Your newfound humility will actually create a charismatic magnetic attraction to you. It is not something you will need to advertise. Your sincere recognition of your faults will radiate from you naturally, and help you win back the one you've lost.

50 *Be Willing to Change and Grow*

Ideally, everyone would want to change and grow better and better continuously. However, pride stops many of us and becomes a stumbling block in our goal to win back someone we've lost. Don't let this happen to you. Anybody who is unwilling to make changes, stagnates. This is certainly not good for a relationship. But the fact is, there is only one person in this world that you can change—you! So reconcile yourself to the fact that if you want your relationship to grow and become better, you must strip yourself of destructive pride and focus on making positive changes in yourself.

Of course, this doesn't mean that change is easy, but this is one of those instances in which you have to make the choice. Should you stay the way you are and risk the permanent loss of the relationship? Or should you attempt to make certain needed changes, which will increase the likelihood of reconciliation? Don't feel that you have to completely change overnight. Make slow but steady changes in a direction that will make you more desirable in the eyes of the one you want to win back.

If you have spent your life resisting change, then facing this need to make some adjustments may make you angry. You might feel that you shouldn't be the one changing, the other person should! Remember, you are the one who is trying to win back the other person. So you are the one who must take the first step. But let us assure you that change is really not so bad. Once you begin the practice of routinely making yourself a better person, you'll find that it actually becomes empowering and fun!

Use a simple plan to make changes. The first step is to analyze specifically what went wrong. Try to be as objective as you can. What are the reasons that led to this relationship dissolving? What have you done or failed to do that resulted in your loved one's dissatisfaction? Remember, being used as a doormat could be as fatal to the relationship as being totally selfish. What were your particular failings? Take a sheet of paper and write down every conceivable idea that comes into your mind.

Once you have a fair idea of what you've done wrong, the next step is trying to figure out what can be done to rectify the problem (and not repeat it). What changes can be made? How can you make certain changes? Again, it is a good idea to jot down all the thoughts that come to mind.

Finally, implement your plan. The best way to do this is simple—don't repeat the mistakes you are now aware of. Don't tell the other person you've changed. Show them. This will take a little time, but it will be most effective in the long run.

51 *Create Some Excitement*

Boredom is often a factor that has caused relationships to fall apart; but it is also one of the many things you can change. One or both individuals in a relationship may have become so locked into certain patterns and routines that the spice is gone. Try to bring some variety and excitement back into the relationship. Don't fall back into the same old rut. Figure out things that will interest and entice the other person. Do new things that will make the one you've lost recognize that change has occurred, and that there are more good things that can still evolve out of the relationship. Try to add a little variety to your everyday life. Don't always go to the same places. Try new restaurants, vacation spots, or even a different skating rink. Don't sit around all the time. Get out of the house. Try cultivating new friends.

Variety is the spice of life! If companionship is the cake, excitement is the icing. So it's essential to create excitement in your relationship by seeking to grow, having new experiences, and being unpredictable.

You take a positive step in your relationship when you try to create excitement and have new experiences. Your efforts will further endear you to the one you want. It's so important that you try, even if you fail in the attempt. A good attitude about trying to develop new experiences in life will cause you to become more attractive.

Excitement can be created in several ways. Having a positive attitude and trying to muster enthusiasm (even when it is not strongly felt) is one way of creating an air of excitement. The one you've lost will recognize your efforts, no matter how feeble, and this will go a long way towards softening their heart and giving the relationship another look.

16

Fixing Communication Skills

Principle: *The more in tune you are with someone, the more he or she will want to be with you.*

---

he biggest part of any relationship is friendship, and the core of friendship is communication. When you're trying to win back the one you have lost, being able to communicate is of utmost importance. Almost always, failure of love is partly due to problems in this area. Therefore, if you want to win this person back, you'll have to look closely at past communication weaknesses.

There's a saying that goes, "Facts not frankly faced have a way of coming back around and stabbing you in the back." That's what happens in a lot of relationships. If you are afraid to communicate frankly and freely, eventually the relationship will fail. Accordingly, you need to have good communication skills, and you need to improve them if they've been the source of losing the one you want.

SO WHAT HAPPENS?

What are some of the ways in which the communication in your relationship has broken down? Conversation may no longer be meaningful because it withholds honest feelings. Usually this is because those involved in the relationship have fallen into destructive practices such as criticizing, judging, and giving advice. Empathy is sometimes forgotten. If good habits are resumed, communication will improve, and loving feelings will be resurrected from the dead.

As communication breaks down in a relationship, it is common to feel vulnerable and resort to defensive behaviors. But this is the very time to repent of bad communication habits that have developed, and make a concerted effort to apply correct principles of listening. Don't worry if the one you're losing or have already lost is not listening yet. If you stay cool, calm, and collected while focusing on empathy as outlined earlier in the book, they will soon begin to respond.

Virtually every single communication-improving tactic found in this book is relevant in trying to win back the one you've lost. You may find it helpful to reread the communication tactics discussed in Part One. Reflective listening skills in Chapter 8 are particularly relevant at this stage, as are the thought-provoking ideas presented in this chapter.

52 *Start a Healing Conversation*

Good communication is an essential key to reestablishing a positive relationship. Sometimes, however, things have gotten so bad that all talk has stopped. Initially, you may have to settle for *any* type of interaction to get the lines of communication back. Don't worry if you feel awkward at first. It's all part of that newfound humility we talked about earlier.

There are times when you may be reluctant to express your feelings because you feel as if you're walking on eggshells. You may fear that if you say anything more it will further damage the relationship. But if you are sincere about eliminating your own tendencies to judge, and you begin to listen with the pure intention of understanding, improvement in the relationship can't help but occur. It may be slow in the beginning, depending on your skill, but *any* effort to apply correct principles will have positive results. As you become more skilled with practice, the pace of progress will increase.

Start a conversation. Say whatever you have to in order to draw out that person's feelings. Try, try, try! Then listen, listen, listen! Withhold criticism and judgment. Try to understand. Be persistent. Show consideration, but be persistent.

Getting a conversation going under these circumstances is like pushing a stopped car. The hardest part is getting it moving in the first place. Once it is moving, though, pushing it becomes a lot easier (in spite of the fact that you may be pushing a two-ton piece of machinery). However, anticipate uphills as well as downhills in these discussions. Don't give up just because you suddenly fall into the old traps momentarily. Just back off long enough to strengthen your resolve to listen without being defensive, and then start again.

53 *Keep Interactions Warm*

Don't be hostile. Avoid being contentious. In your conversational efforts, try to be as calm and as sincerely accepting as you possibly can. The other person may get angry or hostile, but don't let this happen to you. Maintaining control is essential. You're treading on thin ice already; so don't risk sinking into the icy waters where there is no communication at all!

A perfect example of maintaining control comes from an episode of the television classic *The Honeymooners*. Ralph and his wife, Alice, had gotten into a fight in which he called her names. She stormed out of the house and went to live with her mother. Once Ralph had cooled down, he and his good buddy Ed Norton decided to send Alice a recorded message in the hope that she would melt when she heard it and come back to him.

He began the recording by being very warm and loving. However, as the recording continued, he became angrier. He ended the recording by losing control completely, calling Alice some of the very same names that had caused her to storm out!

Norton immediately jumped in and calmed down Ralph, who began a new recording. This time Ralph maintained control and was able to express his feelings in a very loving and endearing way. Even Norton was brought to tears!

Norton was then given the responsibility of delivering the recording to Alice. As you might have guessed, Norton gave Alice the wrong tape. You can imagine the consequences of such a grievous mistake!

So what's the moral? Maintain control. By remaining calm and expressing your feelings in a warm, loving, supportive way, you can increase the likelihood of developing a conversation in which an exchange of ideas is comfortable.

54 ❤ *Understand, Don't Just Agree; Listen, Don't Just Hear*

This tactic relates to giving feedback. When you express agreement or disagreement, you are implying that you understand what the other person is feeling. But that is really not your judgment to make. Only the other person can judge whether or not you are understanding correctly. Your objective is simply to reflect what they are saying in such a way that the one you've lost feels that you're beginning to understand them. You'll know you're accomplishing this by the appreciative look in their eyes, and a pleasantly surprised tone in their voice as they say, "Right," "Exactly," or "You've got it!"

How do you accomplish this? Simply by implementing the reflective listening techniques we talked about in Part One. Briefly, this means attempting to rephrase what the other person is saying, then asking for a confirmation of your understanding. You want the other person to sense that, yes, you're aware of the doubt, the dilemma, the negative feelings that they're experiencing. When they feel you understand them again, the old feelings of love will start to rekindle within them. By experiencing this, they will be reminded of the old bonds that still tie them to you.

Don't become defensive if the other person becomes critical of you. One of the surest ways for the lines of communication to break down is to become defensive and retaliate with painful retorts. Don't do that. Rather, sidestep any verbal javelins that may be thrown your way, allow them to land harmlessly, then respond in a way that is designed to add to and enhance communication.

55 *Keep on Stroking*

Another area that is easy to neglect in a relationship is that of continuing to praise your loved one. You must continue to stroke their ego, no matter how long you have been together. Regardless of the discouragement you may feel in the relationship, be determined to sprinkle in a liberal amount of praise and compliments from time to time. This is a universal need, and without it, humans can become emotionally malnourished. By including a generous amount of praise in your conversations, and by emphasizing the good, positive qualities of the one you've lost, you can increase the likelihood that they will begin again to listen to the other things you have to say. Remembering their need for positive recognition will help you win back the one you have lost.

56 *Insist, Don't Plead*

In your attempts to improve communication while trying to win back the one you've lost, there is one last thing we must add. Don't misunderstand what we've been saying here and become a wimp. Never allow yourself to be disrespected and demeaned. Remain in control of your emotions. Begging or pleading indicates a lack of power and does nothing to gain the respect of the other person. On the other hand, if you firmly insist on being respected, it will not hurt your attempts to win back the one you've lost. A gentle show of confidence may be the very thing to help restore your relationship.

A girl we know, Joanne, came to us for counseling. She described how ideal her love relationship was in some ways, but how frustrating it was in others. Her boyfriend constantly took her for granted. She pleaded with him on numerous occasions to stop taking advantage of her, but he either didn't respond or he blew it off. The behavior continued.

Joanne soon realized that her pleading came across as weak and nagging. She learned that if she really wanted her boyfriend to stop taking advantage of her, she had to *insist* that he stop. And she had to be willing to back up her insistence with a consequence. When you insist on something, you must be prepared to follow up with an actual consequence. And if you're not prepared to follow up, don't nag! It will come across as whiny and create disrespect in the relationship.

Remember, you don't have the right to change someone simply for the sake of change. You do, however, have a real right to insist that the other person does not hurt you in any way.

17

Using Attention Wisely

Principle: *Attending to the needs of the one you want will make them feel valued, and they will draw closer to you.*

One of the most widely used concepts in raising children is that attention affects behavior. Attention is not the only factor, but it is certainly the dominant one.

It's the same with adults. The basis of the human emotional diet is attention. No person can get enough. Therefore, if you provide a person with quality attention, they will blossom and grow in a relationship with you.

57 *Demonstrate the Advantages of You*

Watch any effective sales presentation and notice that the salesperson points out benefit after benefit before mentioning the product's special low price. The price of the product is never given first. It's the same way in relationships. To win back the one you've lost, you're going to have to maximize the benefits to them and minimize the costs.

In the game of love, you should realize that you are selling yourself. You have to show the other person why it is in their best interest to maintain a relationship with you. The operative word here is show, not talk. Telling someone that you love them, care about them, and are committed to them, is not nearly as effective as being in a relationship and showing these things to the person. You should do as little talking and as much showing as possible.

In trying to win someone back, remember that many of the advantages that were initially part of the relationship may have been buried by neglect over time. Part of your strategy should include a good faith demonstration that those positive aspects of the relationship are not dead. They were just forgotten, and now you intend to reestablish them in the relationship.

58 Give Freely of Your Love

There are two kinds of love: unconditional and conditional. Unconditional love is given purely, without expectation of reciprocation. Conditional love is given with the expectation of receiving something in return. Although conditional love is more common, you must be willing to give a certain amount of love unconditionally throughout your life. As the words in the book of Ecclesiastes say, "There is a time and a season to every purpose under heaven." This is also true about love. There is a time for conditional love, and also a time for unconditional love.

The need to give unconditional love is especially important if you're trying to reestablish a relationship. You have to be able to show the person that you have the capacity, the strength, and the desire to give without expecting something in return. And as you do, the other person will open his or her mind to the benefits of reconciling with you.

59 Share Quality Time

The greatest sacrifice you can make to assure a person of your love and commitment is to give of your time. Of course, quality time means positive time. This involves meeting the other person's emotional needs for attention, understanding, acceptance, appreciation, and affection. If you're not meeting those needs, then you're not giving quality time. There is a big difference between quality time and quantity time. Often, the reason a relationship has soured is because quality time was neglected and emotional needs ignored.

To determine what quality time is, take yourself out of your own desires. Focus on the other person. Think of what that other person may have communicated to you in the past. What things did they want from you (time-wise), or did they just want you to be available? And exactly what did that mean to them? This is what defines quality time for them, so this is what you want to offer.

When you decide on things to do, make sure that you are extra sensitive to what you think the other person wants. All too often, one's own interests take precedence. These priorities tend to overwhelm the other person's desires. A relationship can fall apart if a person feels that his or her interests are not being enjoyed. Try to focus as clearly as possible on those important activities, those interesting events that the other person would enjoy. Make yourself an integral part of those activities.

If the one you want to win back has wanted you to try a particular activity for a long period of time, try it. Even if it's something that you never wanted to do before, and even if the other person knows of your lack of interest, sincerely express your interest in trying it.

Quality time often involves being alone with the other person. Larger get-togethers can sometimes take away from that quality time. Time that is spent in constructive discussion, in which thoughts and ideas are shared with one another, is considered quality. Compare this to time spent silently staring at the television or a movie screen. Talking during commercials is not necessarily quality time. But substantive reflective listening, especially if the one you want is hurting, is an example of quality time.

60 *Share Burdens and Responsibilities*

A major motivation for getting married is companionship. The fact is that life is difficult and tough to go through alone. Life is easier when you have someone to share it with. Ponder the Asian saying, "Shared joy is double joy, shared sorrow is half sorrow." Life's joys are more joyful and the lows less painful when they are shared with a true companion. Show the other person your willingness to share not only the joyful experiences but the burdens as well. This can be a very important strategy for winning back the one you have lost.

Be helpful. One of the things that can create a rift in a relationship is the feeling that somebody has to bear his or her burdens alone. Show sensitivity to their feelings and try to bring about change. Try to share the burdens. Find out what the most unpleasant things are for them, and then help out as much as you can. The minimal amount of time that this involves on your part will reap great rewards.

Often in a relationship, both people fall into their own individual routines. This can be fine as long as both are still attuned to each other's needs and are there for each other. But truly sharing each other's burdens and responsibilities requires commitment and vigilance to always remain alert.

18

Being a Successful Competitor

Principle: *Never become discouraged. If things don't work out one way, they will another.*

*I*f you are trying to win back the one you've lost, you may be involved in intense competition. This may be because your former love is no longer interested in you, or because he or she is being pursued by another person.

If the one you want to win back has already entered a relationship with someone else, you will have a much more difficult road to travel. This doesn't mean that your task is impossible, but you have to be aware that the person may be less receptive to your tactics.

There's a saying, "Never let them see you sweat." This would apply when a rival affects your relationship or your efforts at winning back the one you have lost. Remember that those who are capable of looking failure squarely in the face without flinching show true strength.

Ultimately, you must prepare yourself for the possibility of failure, even though you have maximized your possibilities for success by using love tactics. Try not to fear failure. It can be counterproductive to fear the loss of the one you love to another person. It is better to face the always-present possibility that you may lose that person, and know that you'll go on and survive anyway.

Is this negative thinking? No! What you're really doing is trying to strengthen yourself to become ready for these possibilities. And your strength will be conveyed to the one you want. This is much better than making your fear evident, which can actually weaken your possibilities with the other person. Your ability to communicate confidence is one of the strongest elements you can introduce in your attempts to win back the one you want.

Never fear your rival. Always have confidence in the love tactic principles. If you treat the person in the best possible way and meet his or her emotional needs, ultimately you can come out on top.

61 Face Your Rival

You must be able to face your rival in any situation and still show the ability to handle the complete loss of the one you want to that rival. If there is any chance for your success, it is through this course.

If you know who the other love interest is, don't show fear. Don't present yourself as being inferior to that person or in awe of that person. Always show yourself as a pillar of strength.

It's normal to feel jealous. It's normal to feel insecure. It's normal to feel intimidated. But don't speak negatively of your rival to the one you want. Rather, speak of that person respectfully (if you have to refer to them at all).

It's best to just ignore the competitive situation as much as possible. Pretend that you are not affected one way or another. Don't demonstrate jealousy. It will cause the one you want to feel closed in, trapped, and inclined to try to get away from you. Jealous actions won't get you back together.

62 Withhold What They Want

When you feel your partner drawing away from you, it is instinctive to cling tighter. Remember one of the paradoxes of love: People are drawn to that which evades them, and try to escape that which pursues. Making use of this phenomenon of human behavior is often referred to as "reverse psychology," and is applicable in courtship and romance.

This calls to mind the story of the little boy who went with his father to fly a kite. His father showed him how to let the string out so the kite would rise. By the time the string was out all the way, the kite was flying high. The little boy excitedly jumped up and down because he had never seen such a thing before. He said, "Daddy, let the string go. The kite will go all the way up to the sun." The father responded, "If we let the string go, the kite will go off course, fly about wildly, and eventually crash to the ground. Remember, son, sometimes it is the thing that holds you down that keeps you up."

In romance, the same kind of paradox applies. Sometimes, the things you think have an adverse effect on the relationship can actually have a positive effect. So if the other person shows signs of drawing away from you, you may want to draw away from them a bit. Show a little independence. As you do, you will suddenly become more desirable to them.

When trying to restore a relationship, it's very easy to forget this rule, especially at the first sign that the person may be coming back to you. But realize that you must still withhold some of yourself. The more totally you give of yourself, the less desirable you become.

63 *Be Persistent and Consistent*

Persistence is the key to accomplishing all things. Consistency is simply proving your integrity through your behavior and remaining true to the principles that have been presented in this book.

You won't be able to apply the principles perfectly, but you must continue in your efforts to the best of your ability. Learn from your mistakes. Persistence does not mean that you keep trying something that does not work. Rather, try something, evaluate the portion that doesn't work, and learn how to reapply it in a better way. Persistence just says, "I don't give up, I will find a way . . ."

Remember the saying, "Slow and steady wins the race." Don't be abnormally aggressive in any phase of your attempts to win back the one you have lost. Rather, be persistent and consistent. Continue to do the things you feel are going to help your relationship, and show that you are ready, willing, and able to change.

64 *Suggest Conditions for Reconciliation*

Don't suggest conditions for reconciliation before the other person is ready. It may be a turn-off if they feel that you're trying to sew them up, and it may drive them away. The best approach? Give freely of your love until they clearly want you back.

It's probably better to let the other person indicate areas of change that they would like to see. This may be done in a testing manner at first, without any commitment. The implication, however, is that if changes are made, they'll be happier with you and they'll want to be back in a relationship with you.

Remember that throughout all of these discussions your competitor may be lurking in the background, waiting for something to go wrong. Make sure you keep this in mind, especially when you start discussing your own terms for reconciliation.

Sometimes, especially if you're the one trying to win the other person back, you're better making very few demands. Don't give a long list of things that have to be changed. You're in no position to be demanding when you are the one who is on thin ice to start with!

In preparing the groundwork for reconciliation, try to listen very carefully and take very seriously every concern that is expressed by the other person. Don't belittle their concerns. What are the most important things that the person wants from you?

Make sure that *both* of your needs are being addressed. Don't make it seem like everything that's being done is for the other person at this point. You are involved, too! Don't become a doormat.

It's very important not to press for a commitment. Reflect the other person's feelings back to them. Then follow up on their suggestions by showing your acceptance and understanding through your behavior. Through your actions, show that you're actually making the changes they had hoped for. Let them know that you're really listening to them and sensitive to their needs.

Continue to focus on the reasons for the split so that you can make sure the same mistakes don't happen again. Part of the conditions of your reconciliation may be to have continued discussions that focus on the areas of your incompatibility. It may take some time before the other person is willing to take a chance on a commitment with you again. Remember that positive things existed in the original relationship, and you must try to reestablish them.

All of the tactics we've described need to be continued in a successful ongoing relationship. Don't feel as if the only way that there can be reconciliation is by doing everything for the other person. Yes, you must be willing to change, but a good strong relationship requires flexibility, compromise, and willingness on both sides. So, while striving to meet the other person's needs, don't allow them to walk all over you in the process.

If there seems to be a desire to reconcile, make sure that you maintain a long-term perspective in which all efforts are focused on that reconciliation. Try not to plan on an immediate full reconciliation. In other words, don't say to yourself, "We'll be back together in a week." You can be sure that there will be some problems that will occur after a week.

Try to focus on a reconciliation effort of six months or longer in which both people must work to overcome the obstacles that set the relationship apart in the first place. Remember, the relationship did not go bad overnight (although it may have seemed to). It will take awhile to recultivate the relationship.

In your discussions on reconciliation (or on anything for that matter), sound confident and constructive in the things you say. Don't whine or beg. This behavior won't inspire interest from the other person.

65 *Give the Other Person a Vacation from You*

Sometimes, after all you have done or attempted to do, it may seem like you're not finding success. At this point, you may need to let the other person experience life without you. Let that person realize that you're capable of living happily without them. Give them a vacation from you.

This doesn't mean you're giving up. What it does mean is that there's a limit to how much you can continue to bang your head against the wall. If you back off for a while, the other person will become more open to a new encounter with you. A vacation from you will tend to open their eyes to what they're missing.

This vacation can be a week, a month, or even longer, depending on your particular situation. Don't ever feel that this is the end. Make this a specific strategy in which you plan how much time will elapse before your next contact. Prepare yourself for how you'll respond if the person contacts you, and what you plan to do the next time you contact them. Your whole purpose in doing this is to show the person how incomplete his or her life will be without you in it.

66 Consider a Professional, Third-Party Viewpoint

There may be times when, despite everything you've tried to do, you don't succeed. Or you may find that although your relationship might be salvageable, you're not able to do it yourself.

Getting professional help can be a great asset at a time when it seems like nothing else is working. Objective feedback from a trained professional may help you to eliminate the last obstacles that may be keeping you from winning the one you want. Besides, we all need moral support, and sometimes it's just plain nice to know we have someone on our side! If you do seek professional help, make sure you work with somebody who is qualified and experienced in the field of human relationships.

67 Evaluate Who Is Winning the Game

Don't take it personally when the one you want seems unable to respond to your romantic overtures because they're already preoccupied with another love interest. When a person is already involved in another fulfilling love relationship, it does not leave a lot of room for your pursuit.

What it all comes down to, though, is how successful your rival suitor is in his or her ability to satisfy all three of the fundamental romance needs of friendship, respect, and passion in the life of your mutual love object. Realistically, your competitor is at a disadvantage, unless he or she has also read *Love Tactics*.

Until the one you want is married, anything is still possible. However, as a practical matter, if the one you want is already in love with someone who is doing a fairly good job of meeting their basic love needs of friendship, respect, and passion, then that relationship is fairly secure for your rival. Don't be discouraged by your seeming powerlessness in a situation like this. It doesn't mean that you are an inferior rival, or that you are unable to apply love tactics skillfully. It is simply a matter of arriving on the scene after the window of opportunity is tightly closed. Yes, it can be a bit painful, but be assured that there are others who will be inspired by your ardor.

This is the one situation in which your best alternative may be to find someone new. Yes, some people actually do choose to wait it out indefinitely, but we recommend that you look for someone else. Focus on the future. There are other options.

Remember, there was one person you wanted, and there will be others. There's nothing wrong with beginning again. And what's more, you have *Love Tactics* to help you from the beginning!

68 Don't Settle for a Relationship That Requires Force

If you work hard enough, there isn't anyone you can't ultimately win over. But beyond a wholesome application of the principles outlined in this book, don't attempt to force the one you want to respond the way you need them to, or you'll be sorry. If you have to go beyond reasonable efforts to achieve your goal from the start, it is an indication that things are not going to run smoothly later on. You will probably spend the rest of your life fighting to keep your head above water.

Some time ago, real estate magnate Donald Trump wanted to purchase the Plaza Hotel in New York City. He *had to have it,* and he was willing to pay more for the hotel than it was worth. Because he was carried away with the emotion of wanting, instead of thinking things out logically, the normally clear-thinking Trump broke his own rule and overpaid for the hotel. The Plaza's expenses eventually exceeded its income and helped create a crisis in Trump's financial empire.

The same type of thing can happen in the pursuit of a love relationship. The costs of the relationship, in terms of emotional output, can sometimes far outstrip the emotional rewards. You may win the person but lose the battle for a fulfilling life, so be careful. You can't change the basic nature of the one you want simply by capturing that person's heart (and don't ever fool yourself into thinking otherwise). Do your best to make a relationship work, but don't feel obligated to go beyond that. Don't force it. In emotional terms, make a fair offer by doing the things this book suggests, but if the other person remains hesitant about meeting your emotional needs, then seriously consider withdrawing from the relationship altogether.

The most rewarding, fulfilling relationship you can ever experience is the one that allows you to stretch your capacities and skills to make it work, but not to the point that makes you snap. Be willing to throw in the towel if the other person's heart requires extreme measures on your part to stimulate a loving response. It is a sign that their ability to meet your ongoing emotional needs is too underdeveloped and conditional to ever bring you the fulfillment and happiness you deserve (even if they do marry you). It is an unhealthy obsession for you to stay involved in a relationship that cannot and will not bring you the consummate fulfillment that you desire. The greatest happiness results from choosing someone who not only keeps you on your toes, but who also gives you the love you need in return for the love you give.

Sometimes the difference between choosing someone who loves you enough to meet your needs and someone who does not may be razor thin, but it makes a world of difference in the ultimate outcome. In business, you must show a profit, which you can't do with continual losses. It is the same in romance. Emotional deficits will eventually result in romantic bankruptcy.

For you to make a good decision, you must be emotionally strong enough to "take it or leave it," based on the objective assessment of whether or not you can get a fair return of love on your investment of time and self. Cutting your losses and changing pursuit of an object are not indications of your inabilities, but of a realistic assessment of the maturity level of the one you want. You can win their conditional love, but if they don't have an adequate supply of unconditional love to meet your needs *then you just ain't gonna get it!*

Do what is right, then let the consequences follow. The irony of finding the inner strength to let a bad relationship go is that you will be able to find true love so much more easily. There is someone out there who is really good for you, someone who can bring you a sense of fulfillment and great happiness. Don't compromise and settle. Wait for the "right" person—one who is able to give you the love you need.

Frank Bettger, a phenomenal salesman of the 1930s, shared the secret of his success in his classic *How I Raised Myself from Failure to Success in Selling*. After analyzing his first year's sales, Bettger discovered that 70 percent were made on the first interview, 23 percent on the second interview, and 7 percent on the third. His greatest revelation was that he spent half of his time going after that last 7 percent! When he realized this, he began concentrating his efforts on those first interviews and nearly doubled his income overnight!

In similar fashion, when pursuing the love of your life, you should be willing to let go when it's obvious that your needs for loving attention are not being met after you've made a reasonable effort to love the person the best you can. What's reasonable? When you have pretty much exhausted your best understanding of the principles in this book.

If you're spending all your time trying to carve a square peg to go through a round hole, it's just not worth the effort. We assure you that the world is full of round pegs just waiting for you. And don't feel obligated to take one that you don't want! If a blue peg is what you want, then don't settle for a green or a yellow. Keep sorting until you find your blue peg. But don't get stuck on a square peg just because it's blue. It may cause you to miss your opportunity for a partner who has everything, including the ability to meet your very real emotional needs.

We have interviewed many people who have spent years fruit-lessly trying with all their might to make an existing relationship work. After finally cutting their losses and going on alone, they even-tually met someone else. This was not because the pursuer had sud-denly become more attractive or smarter. He or she wasn't working any harder at the relationship; however, the pursuer was now relat-ing with a person who was mature enough to appreciate his or her qualities.

Don't fall for the misconception that once you lose someone, you will never be able to find anyone else you'll want as much. It may require some scratching in the barnyard, but there *are* more "pickin's" out there!

In summary, give it your best. Do your part to cultivate a rela-tionship with the one you want. But if experience proves that he or she remains hardhearted even after you have given it your all, then wish them the best and get on with finding somebody who *will* recip-rocate your love after a reasonable effort. True love is still waiting out there for you.

69 *Proceed with Faith*

The one element that we have saved for last is, for many, the most important. Let your life be guided by faith. It is comforting to believe that all of life's experiences are part of a greater plan. Successes and accomplishments, as well as disappointments, all add color and tex-ture to the tapestry of your life.

Believe in the strength of a higher power that is armed with goodness and a loving hand to guide you purposefully through life. Trust in God. By believing that everyday happenings are not without design or reason, you will gain strength and confidence when facing challenges.

In all areas, including love, have faith that each twist and turn has a purpose. Believe that a seemingly negative experience can bring about something positive, and keep in mind that when one door closes, another one opens.

If you maintain a strong faith and trust that there is a purpose for the things you experience, it will be easier to overcome any difficulties. Remember that any suffering you may encounter along life's way is only temporary and, in some way, may be the cause of future happiness.

Final Words

*I*f there is one overriding theme of this work, it is that love does not just happen. It has to be cultivated. When this truth finally sinks into your heart, it will open a new world of unlimited power to you.

A person who is truly in love experiences about 90 percent friendship, 9 percent respect, and about 1 percent passion for the other person (although it is that 1 percent of which we are most conscious). Ideally, both people in a relationship should feel this balance toward each other.

Although 100 percent passion may be exciting for a short while, it's not enough. If the core of your relationship is not friendship, where you can count on your long-term emotional needs being met, you will eventually become as sick as a kid who eats nothing but icing from a birthday cake. Icing is nice, but not when you make an entire meal out of it. We want you to have your cake and eat it, too!

If you get nothing else from this book, let it be this: Every time you utilize a love tactic principle, you'll be creating a more positive relationship than you had before. As long as you do something to further cultivate one of the areas of friendship, respect, or passion, you cannot help but improve the love between you. And even if this improvement is not enough to elicit the commitment you want today, keep working on it. Someday it will be.

While this book has explored various methods of cultivating each of the three important elements of love, it's up to you to evaluate your current relationship and zero in on what it lacks. If the one you want enjoys your friendship but mistreats you and seems to take you for granted, then you need to take steps to increase the respect in the relationship.

On the other hand, if the other person fears more than trusts you, then concentrate on doing things to improve friendship. Remember to cultivate what you lack in the relationship. It can be only as strong as its weakest link in this three-link chain.

You may not need a lot of passion, but you do need some. Frankly, though, this should be your lowest priority in building a successful relationship. You shouldn't worry about getting the one you want crazy with passion until everything else is in place first. Then, when the friendship is solid, and the respect is firmly established, you can ignite the whole powder keg in one fell swoop. This will forever after be known as "the moment he [she] fell in love with you."

So there you have it! The formula of the ages. Practice these principles and they will enrich your life immeasurably. It is the fondest wish of the authors that you have a happier life through their application.

The overall philosophy of *Love Tactics* can best be summed up in the poetic words of Emmet Fox:

Love

There is no difficulty that enough love will not conquer; no disease that enough love will not heal; no door that enough love will not open; no gulf that enough love will not bridge; no wall that enough love will not throw down, no sin that enough love will not redeem.

It makes no difference how deeply seated may be the trouble, how hopeless the outlook, how muddled the tangle, how great the mistake; a sufficient realization of love will dissolve it all. If only you could love enough you would be the happiest and most powerful being in the world.

Dr. Emmet Fox, "Love Card" (Marina del Rey, Calif.: DeVorss Publications). Used by permission of the publisher.

We wish you the best in your quest for love. It is the greatest crusade a man or woman can embark upon in this world. Good luck with *Love Tactics*! As you apply these principles in your life, you'll become increasingly convinced—as we are—of their effectiveness in winning the one you want.

The many love tactics offered in this book have been presented in a way that we hope will enhance your efforts in winning the one you want or winning back the one you've lost. It is virtually impossible to cover every possible variable that may occur, each scenario that may exist, or every obstacle that you may encounter. If you have any questions or a particular problem for which you'd like some additional guidance, please feel free to write to us in care of the publisher. We'd be happy to hear from you. Please share your successes with us as well. The greatest reward any author can receive is knowing how much his or her book has helped someone.

About the Authors

Thomas W. McKnight is a 1977 graduate of Brigham Young University. He and his wife, the former Gaylynn Grover, live in Las Vegas, Nevada, where he has been a Social Worker with the Division of Child and Family Services since 1979.

Mr. McKnight is a human relations expert and lecturer who writes and speaks on the subject of romantic love. The insights he shares in this book are drawn from many of his own observations as a single in the dating world, as well as from the many experiences confided to him by other singles anxiously engaged in "the quest." His books, *Love Tactics: How to Win the One You Want* and *More Love Tactics: How to Win That Special Someone,* have been perennial bestsellers throughout the world since 1988, and are now published in more than a dozen languages.

A veteran of *The Oprah Winfrey Show, The Jenny Jones Show, Regis & Kathy Lee, CNN Newsnight,* and over a hundred television and radio shows across the United States and Canada, Mr. McKnight wrote a weekly column for the *National Singles Register* for over a decade in the late 1980s and early 1990s. He served a mission for the Church of Jesus Christ of Latter-Day Saints from 1973 to 1975.

Robert H. Phillips, Ph.D., is a practicing psychologist on Long Island, New York. He is the founder and director of the Center for Coping, a multi-service organization offering private and group counseling to help individuals cope with a variety of situations.

The author of twenty-five books on how to deal with various chronic health conditions, Dr. Phillips has also written numerous articles on a variety of subjects in the field of psychology. He has lectured at conventions, universities, and professional meetings throughout the country, and has appeared on local and national radio and television programs. Currently he is the host of a weekly radio show on Long Island, New York.